The Smart Couple's Guide to

"In my nineteen years as a wedding ph_____ ___es miss out on the spiritual and romant_____ng should be about. I am thrilled to recommend this _____se it can rescue all future brides from making the same mistake."

— Wilson Pinilla, president and CEO, Pinilla Photography and Video Inc.

"Practical, prescient, precious. Judith and Jim have created a wedding masterpiece!"

— Pat Love, EdD, author of *The Truth about Love*

"The wedding market is flooded with how-to books — planners that all say essentially the same thing. Finally, here is a new and interesting approach. This is a book for the modern couple, reflecting the growing trend of the groom's involvem_____wedding planning ___y can be — should be — the _____

— Gerard _____Consultants

"From 'Popping _____rything in between, this boo_____and future daughter-in-law _____

— Charlie Bloom, coauthor of
101 Things I Wish I Knew When I Got Married

"This book is a joy to read from cover to cover. Every bride and groom need to read it so they can enjoy planning their wedding while also building the basis for the success of their future marriage."

— Susan Jeffers, PhD, author of *Feel the Fear and Do It Anyway* and
The Feel the Fear Guide to Lasting Love

"In this beautiful and sensible book, Doctors Judith and Jim have outlined a remarkable blueprint that will save couples time and money. The spiritual principles will help them to create deeper intimacy as they transition from twoness to oneness."

— Dr. Grace Cornish, bestselling author of *The Sacred Bond*

"This practical, helpful book guides couples through perhaps the most important event of their lives to date and makes the experience more joyful than they imagined."

— Brian Tracy, author of *Create Your Own Future*

"This absolutely great book is a fascinating, readable, and wise blend of romance and practicality! From the earliest considerations of engagement to the end of the honeymoon, this book is an amazing gift to those couples who want to make their marriage and their lives reflect their souls."

— Sidra Stone, PhD, and Hal Stone, PhD, cocreators of Voice Dialogue and authors of *Partnering* and *Embracing Our Selves*

"Utilizing real couples' stories and their own rich experiences, Judith and Jim brilliantly lead you through the rocky terrain of getting married, from preengagement considerations to the wedding day and beyond. Throughout, they act as the little voice in your head gently urging you to be true to yourself by planning a ceremony that will genuinely reflect the bond between you and your beloved. I will, without hesitation, recommend this book to all my nervous brides-to-be."

— Farah Husain, bridal makeup artist

"Too often, men are encouraged to leave the wedding planning to their fiancées — with the result that their weddings and their marriages suffer. From a refreshing and very inspiring point of view, Judith and Jim reveal why it's essential for the bride and groom to plan their wedding together. This book establishes the template for weddings of the future."

— Melissa Wilt, public policy analyst, Men's Health Network

"This book is hard to put down! Filled with invaluable information, it's everything a couple needs to plan their wedding and their life together."

— Richard Markel, president, Association for Wedding Professionals International, and founder, Bridal Show Producers International

"Judith and Jim give couples the tools to discover what matters most to them for their ceremony and its various celebrations, opening the door to rich communication, which is the basis for a strong marriage."

— Julia Markel, vice-president, Association for Wedding Professionals International

"As a wedding gown designer whose main concern is that the bride receive maximum value, I applaud Judith and Jim's practical, enthusiastic guide showing the wedding couple how to maximize the value and meaning of every aspect of their journey into marriage."

— Madeline Gardner, designer of bridal gowns, Mori Lee LLC

The Smart *Couple's* Guide
to the *Wedding* of Your Dreams

Other Books by Judith & Jim

Be Loved for Who You Really Are

*The New Intimacy: Discovering the Magic
at the Heart of Your Differences*

Opening to Love 365 Days a Year

The Smart *Couple's* Guide
to the *Wedding* of Your Dreams

⚹

Planning *Together* for
Less Stress and More *Joy*

Judith Sherven *&* James Sniechowski

New World Library
Novato, California

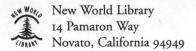

New World Library
14 Pamaron Way
Novato, California 94949

Text design and typography by Tona Pearce Myers

Library of Congress Cataloging-in-Publication Data
Sherven, Judith.
The smart couple's guide to the wedding of your dreams : planning together for less stress and more joy / Judith Sherven and James Sniechowski.
    p.   cm.
Includes index.
ISBN 1-57731-341-0 (pbk. : alk. paper)
1. Weddings—Planning. I. Sniechowski, James. II. Title.
HQ745.S59 2005
395.2'2—dc22   2005016308

g A proud member of the Green Press Initiative

First printing, December 2005
ISBN-10: 1-57731-341-0
ISBN-13: 978-1-57731-341-X

Printed in Canada on partially recycled paper
Distributed by Publishers Group West

10   9   8   7   6   5   4   3   2   1

Contents

ACKNOWLEDGMENTS

With Our Appreciation...

This book was born during a lovely dinner on a snowy evening in upstate New York. We were absorbed in an exciting and intense conversation with our friends Art and Pat about how meaningful and moving our own weddings had been. We shared how the wedding process — from the engagement through the ceremony and reception to the honeymoon — had helped each of us prepare for life as part of a married couple.

After we returned home that evening, we talked about the fact that most people never think to look at the wedding journey as the time when the foundation is set for how the bride and groom will treat each other after they're married. Instead, "wedding fever" (and its negative fallout) is often taken for granted. Then it dawned on us. We'd found the topic for our next book — *this* book.

A few months later, we were in Toronto, chatting about weddings with Rita DeMontis, the lifestyle editor at the *Toronto*

Sun. She was so supportive of our ideas that she asked us to write a feature article, "Wedding Wake-Up Call — I Dos and I Don'ts," in which we sketched out some of the ideas that made their way into this book.

Every time we appeared on radio or television and shared our ideas, the host told us that our message was sorely needed. And countless listeners called in, asking when our book would be available. We kept seeing a sincere and serious need for a book that went beyond the technicalities of wedding planning — invitations, party favors, color schemes, and so on — and into the meaning and spirit of the wedding itself, and did so whether a couple had six hundred or a million dollars to spend.

So we decided to launch a nationwide survey of hundreds of couples about their own weddings to discover how they made their wedding process into a personally meaningful journey. The generosity of the many men and women who responded to our survey touched us deeply and convinced us that it was time to write this book. We are also grateful to the following wedding websites — www.usabride.com, www.weddingchannel.com, and www.ultimatewedding.com — for the online stories that we pass along in these pages.

The continued support and understanding of our friends and family cannot be measured. They were there for us and with us during those months when we spent long days writing and not connecting much with them. For that, and for reviewing the initial drafts of this book and offering their opinions and recommendations, we are indebted to Melody Starr, Beth Davis, Elizabeth Asunsolo, Sondra Clark, Lorraine Seidel, Anni Hartley, Terry Sherven, Kelly Cline, and Bill Sniechowski.

Then there's Peg Booth, our extraordinary publicist, who suggested we take this book to New World Library. You were right, Peg! Thanks so much for your wisdom and guidance.

We deeply appreciate the gentle and caring work done by New World Library's acting managing editor Elizabeth Raphael. Her respect for our project and her engaging humor made working with her a joy.

That brings us to our brilliant and visionary editor at New World Library, Georgia Hughes. Georgia helped us take this book from proposal to the joyous and inspirational read that it is today. We thank you, Georgia, for your tender prodding as well as your trusted nudge to cut the excess.

There are no words to convey our pleasure in and gratitude to the many people who chose to share themselves with you in the following pages. Reading their stories as they arrived through email (sometimes unsolicited by us but encouraged by a mutual friend or acquaintance), we were often moved to tears and/or laughter. And we were always impressed with the tender care and wisdom that flowed through their words. As you will see, each contributor believes in the sanctity of marriage. And each one, men and women alike, participated because they wanted you to have the very best wedding possible.

We are so appreciative of everyone who fueled the fires of our intention to write this book. We hope that it fulfills the desire men and women share to have weddings that reflect their real-life love and their deepest romantic commitment. Therefore, on behalf of everyone who helped bring this book to life, we wish you the wedding of your dreams — your dearest, richest, sweetest, and most meaningful dreams.

A Note from Judith & Jim

We never even talked about it. We just knew we'd create our wedding together. It was so much fun, figuring out what really mattered and what didn't. Everything we did was memorable, another step in actually getting married. Then, when we said our vows, I looked into Ray's eyes and saw him tear up as he told me how much he loved me. I was touched to my soul.

— Deirdre, surgical nurse

Your wedding journey — throughout the planning and preparation — can be a time of great romance and joyous fun, and it can help you to build the foundation for a truly fabulous marriage. We assure you that this is not only possible, it can be the time of your life. In this book, we offer you an approach that will make your journey deeply meaningful — from getting engaged, if you aren't already, through your ceremony, honeymoon, and beyond.

When you create your wedding together as a smart couple, you'll find that:

❖ *planning your wedding can be a close and loving time together;*

❖ *you'll both feel relaxed and excited about your ceremony and reception because you've fully participated and delighted in all the preparations;*

❖ *you'll be proud of the celebration you've created because it will be a true and meaningful expression of the two of you, separately and together;*

❖ *your honeymoon will be far more intimate and romantic than you ever imagined;*

❖ *and you can do all this with less hassle and more joy than the traditional wedding-planning process offers.*

This book is about you — both bride and groom — and the love that creates and supports your vision of your own wedding. The important point here is how *you* want *your* wedding to be. After all, it is your wedding, meant for both of you.

We know you might already feel anxious, stressed out, or worried. Maybe the two of you have started to argue, or you're panicked about how to deal with one or more of your parents. Perhaps you're concerned that you might lose the thread of romance that you thought would take you all the way to the altar. After all, you've heard stories of brides-to-be going to pieces and grooms-to-be going out for beer. This is a time when you need all the comfort and support you can find. Yet it's also a time that offers you great opportunities for creativity and freedom. Our years of professional experience in guiding couples through their wedding process have helped us to understand how you, as a couple, can stay on course: by making your relationship the centerpiece of your plans. Your relationship is the dearest treasure the two of you share. When you place your relationship at the heart of every step you take as you make your way to the altar, your love will support and guide you. You'll discover the deeper meaning and value of your journey from your engagement through your ceremony and reception to your honeymoon and on into your married life.

Throughout the book, we invite you to explore the beauty and freedom that are available when you create your wedding as a team — bride and groom together — on your own terms and guided by your own authority. We assure you that when you commit to discovering the specifics that will make your special day truly perfect, you will have a fabulously fun, genuinely intimate, failure-proof guide for every decision you'll make on your journey together.

Historically, couples have had little freedom to design their own weddings. Etiquette manuals and religious dictates limited their participation. But in recent years, calls for change have risen from many quarters, including the press and wedding professionals. Rather than getting lost in wedding fever, more couples are letting their love lead and making choices that reflect their own personalities and values. Instead of merely complying with the rituals of the past, each of these couples is choosing to express their own vision — a vision that reflects the unique couple that they are.

Through this book we share with you the same advice we've given to each couple who wanted their special day to be their own version of the "perfect" wedding. We talk about our own wedding ceremony, which we invented seventeen years ago and enjoyed so much that we've been working ever since to help make each wedding more suitable to the desires and differences of each couple. And we include stories from dozens of couples who let their love lead in all their choices and created weddings that were far more joyous and heartfelt than they had anticipated — for them as well as for their guests.

To assist you in achieving the same goals, this book asks you a number of important questions that, in the frenzy of conventional wedding planning, often go unanswered. Your answers will keep you focused on the values that are important to you — as individuals and as a couple — and will inspire you to create not just your own wedding day, but also a solid foundation for your future relationship. In this way, ongoing intimacy and true partnership can become more than mere hope. They unite to become the spiritual reality of your life together.

Each chapter guides you through an essential element of your wedding journey. We offer you new perspectives on old traditions — everything from your invitations to your prewedding parties to ways to celebrate your guests — and advice on how to relate to each other once you're alone on your honeymoon. We suggest new alternatives for you to consider as you address the serious choices and rich experiences you'll face together. Rather than merely following tradition or copying what you've seen or read about, you can open your imagination to deeply romantic and powerfully significant possibilities that are uniquely and reassuringly your own.

Through stories from couples who generously shared their magical wedding experiences with us — as well as a few of our own — you'll see that your wedding journey can be a loving rehearsal for a cooperative, power-sharing, and passionately adventuresome marriage. How you treat each other on this journey will establish a pattern for how you will treat each other after you are married.

We interviewed hundreds of people for this book — brides and grooms as well as wives, husbands, and couples. While you will meet only a small number of them in these pages, we extend our gratitude to all of them for their care and generosity of spirit. Some people quoted here felt comfortable with being mentioned only by their first names, while others wanted their entire names used. We changed names and altered details in all stories offered by our clients. We found that the range of wedding preferences was enormous. One couple had no invited guests at their ceremony, while another entertained eight hundred. However, the size of most weddings ranged between fifty and two hundred guests. Several couples spent far less than a thousand dollars on their wedding, while a few others accepted financial help to create luxurious galas. No matter their differences, all these couples had one thing in common — each created their own wedding as a team. And they wouldn't have had it any other way.

This book is not a wedding planner in the conventional sense. For the most part, we do not focus on the details of the wedding itself, but on the choices and values underlying the details of your shared experience. If you're planning a formal ceremony and reception, we trust that you're using any of a number of standard planning guides that are already on the market. And, if you're planning a sizable and complex ceremony and reception, we encourage you to work with a reputable professional wedding coordinator to ensure that your wedding day will go smoothly, leaving you free to be celebrated and honored at your festivities.

While this book focuses on heterosexual couples, we want to make sure that, if you are a same-sex couple, this book is just as relevant to your needs and desires. It is also very helpful for vow-renewal ceremonies.

When you join as a team and consciously cocreate your wedding, you place yourselves squarely at the center of your intentions and follow your own vision, whether you want a traditional or unique and innovative ceremony. And when you do that, you can both truly rejoice in the wedding of your dreams.

The Smart *Couple's* Guide
to the *Wedding* of Your Dreams

CHAPTER I

When It's All about the Two of You

My husband and I planned everything together, down to the tiniest detail, and we discussed everything. By making sure we kept our love front and center, we had an awesome time doing it all! Later we realized it was invaluable practice for planning the rest of our life together.

— Laurie Stevens, high school teacher, Idaho

What's most important to you — impressing your guests, outdoing your cousin, or falling in love with each other again and again before and all through your wedding day and honeymoon? While the answer might seem simple, even obvious, many elements of the traditional wedding could prevent your love from being at the very top of your priority list.

Traditionally, the bride was expected to join with her mother to plan and make all preparations for the wedding day. While this practice might have made sense historically (as we will discuss later), it denies the deep meaning of modern-day marriage between two freely consenting adults. How? By establishing very different roles and responsibilities for the bride and groom, keeping the groom on the outskirts of his own important transition, setting a poor precedent for how the couple will relate to each other once the hoopla is over.

Art, now happily married after a ceremony he designed with his new wife, Pat, speaks not only for millions of grooms who were left out of planning their own weddings, but also for countless brides who missed sharing the experience with the men they loved: "The first time I married, I felt like I was in the way.... Everything up to and including the wedding had nothing to do with support for the marriage we were committing to. In fact, our relationship — the whole point — was never even mentioned as the centerpiece of the event. Instead, the topics were how large a wedding [to have], what kinds of details were necessary to make it impressive, the social status of our choice of honeymoon location, and so on."

Such stories illustrate why we are encouraged to see more and more couples breaking free from automatic expectations about weddings. By claiming authority to create their weddings on their own terms, they are turning the entire process into a loving adventure.

We're delighted that you are claiming your readiness to jointly discover the elements that will make your wedding your own. You can design your wedding to be truly perfect, and that is precisely what we want for you. And that is what we are dedicated to helping you do.

The Perfect Wedding

The words *perfect* and *wedding* just seem to go together, don't they? It's almost as if they are a natural pair. After all, when the two of you say "I do" and commit yourselves to each other, you will be fulfilling an intrinsic and necessary biological drive. You also will be following the spiritual inspiration that draws a man and woman to unite for the purpose of their growth and development as human beings. That is not to be taken lightly. In fact, a moment of such enormous significance *should* be perfect.

However, the word *perfect*, rather than suggesting the radiance and wonder of the wedding promise, often pressures a bride to suffer more stress, more worry, more fear, and more aggressive competition with other brides than she would if she wasn't obsessed with perfection. She feels more of a need to control and is anxious about losing control, which sabotages her enjoyment of the wedding day and the planning that leads up to it. Finally, on what might be the only day of its kind in her life, she's exhausted. As one bride, Maureen, told us, "I couldn't wait to have it all over with. I just wanted to kick off my shoes and soak in a hot bath."

What's the purpose of all that effort? Shouldn't it be your transformation into husband and wife? Isn't that the meaning of marriage and the reason that you're calling everyone together to join in celebration?

Rather than fret over what might be "perfect" pew decorations, reception centerpieces, or favors for your guests, focus on expressing the love you share. That's the deep inspiration for what you are doing; that's what the moment of marriage is all about. Rather than losing yourselves in the impulse to outdo or copy what everyone else is doing, listen to your hearts. Listen to your most private yearnings. Confide in each other — what you're thinking, what you're feeling, what you're afraid of, and what delights you. Discuss your highest vision of your marriage and everything preceding it. The perfection you're looking for will emerge when you share your deepest truths.

Perfection suggests completion. However, the experience of completion will mean something different to each of you. During the busy time leading up to the big day, it's essential that you share not only the details of how you want your ceremony and reception to look and feel, but also the details of how you want to honor the love you share. By opening yourselves you can move beyond the obvious to discover the type of wedding you truly desire, and you will be establishing your readiness for married life.

Talk about your impressions, your intuitions, and your dreams for your wedding day. It doesn't matter how specific or vague, how seemingly petty or grandiose, your thoughts might be. What matters is that you both make space for a jointly created understanding of all that your wedding means to you. Allow a picture of your perfect wedding to emerge, an image that takes its shape from the input you each contribute, an image that will change and evolve as you proceed together. That most privately held image is your richest and best source of inspiration as you determine the "perfect" wedding for the two of you.

For Jeff and Diane, the perfect wedding was, as Diane wrote to us, "actually very funny. Jeff is a stand-up comedian, and I had just written a popcorn cookbook, *For Popcorn Lovers Only* (see www.GritsBits.com). So the whole affair centered around a surprise popcorn wedding ring, a three-tiered popcorn wedding cake that I made, and a popcorn wedding bouquet, and the guests threw... popcorn. I made a three-tiered replacement cake to show on *Regis & Kathie Lee* later that year." Jeff and Diane honored the humor that is so important to them by making it the inspiration for their perfect wedding.

Brian Garcia and his bride, Melanie Hodge, created their event together as an important part of their image of perfection.

Like many men and women we talked with, Brian was pleased that grooms are finally getting attention as active and dedicated wedding partners. He said, "It's about time we men got a little press." Although the stereotype that men aren't interested in things such as wedding planning endures, countless grooms and husbands gave us evidence to the contrary. James Rocknowski wrote, "All the pressure that's put on the couple (or the couple puts on each other) to plan a 'perfect' wedding to mainly benefit those who attend takes away from the spirituality, the true meaning, and the magical moments of the wedding ceremony. Couples get too wrapped up in all the details and miss the soulfulness of the event."

The Payoffs of Doing It Together

During your wedding journey, and especially on the day of your wedding, you don't want to be worried and frazzled about last-minute details. You want to feel confident in the choices you've made — that you've selected the right location, the right style of wedding and reception, and the right support team to take care of you. You want to know that your wedding is everything you dreamed it would be. And you want to know that it is a true expression of you as a couple.

When you join together right from the beginning and commit to using your love as the guiding light for all that you do, you will know that your wedding is for the two of you — not your families or friends or anyone else. You will have the strength to reject the unnecessary and sometimes illness-causing tension that has been a notorious part of weddings.

Rick shared the tension-filled turf war that erupted when he and his fiancée argued about who would be in their wedding party:

BRIDE: "This is *my* wedding!"

GROOM: "Don't you mean *our* wedding?"

BRIDE: *"No!* It's *my* wedding!"

Although Rick and his wife are still married, millions of people who lost sight of their relationships over similar issues are not.

Engaged in the Process

If you've already announced your engagement, you probably discovered that you were immediately pressured to plan and prepare for your wedding. But what will support you as a couple through the many months of planning and preparation to come?

For your engagement to hold its meaning beyond the moment — beyond "Will you marry me?" and "Yes!" — you must keep in mind that you are forging a partnership that will ground your life together. Your commitment, then, has to be made visible through your attitude and actions, not only to your family and friends but to each other. Your engagement is not merely the ring and the announcement; it is the first step in the process that allows you to progressively marry each other all along the way.

Sincere partnership will transform your wedding journey into a time of mutual discovery. You'll find out new information about yourselves and about each other, and you'll discover how well equipped you are to actually work together. That will mean that you will both be changed by the process. After all, through your dedication to bettering your relationship, you will each influence the other. Change will be inevitable. Part of the deep satisfaction of a relationship that succeeds into marriage is finding ways to extend yourself beyond mere tolerance of the differences between you and to broaden your capacity to delight in who you each are. You'll learn to understand your partner's point of view as you recognize, acknowledge, and treasure the magic of your differences.

When you open yourself to the adventure of emotional and spiritual romance with each other, your discoveries will be ongoing. Your teamwork will open the door to a wedding journey filled with fun, joy, and even the wonder of silliness. And, when things get frazzled, your partner will be there with comfort and relief. Through it all, you'll balance each other, setting the tone and style for your married life.

A True Initiation

We humans do not truly understand something, be it an idea, a feeling, a situation, or another person, until we actually have experienced it. Only through experience can we be transformed. Experience gives us an appreciation that cannot be had otherwise. The same is true of your wedding journey. The decisions you make and the manner in which you make them reveal the rich significance of your choice of each other, initiating you into a new way of life. For example, Todd's ideas about family, as he told us, were transformed significantly after he became involved with Wendy:

> I come from a highly dysfunctional family — psychological traumas waited around every turn. Years ago, I decided that I had to distance myself from these destructive patterns, so I broke off all contact with my relatives.
>
> Then came marriage. All of a sudden, I found myself with a family for the first time in over a decade. On a rational level, I knew that not all families are a constant

9

source of pain, but all I had to draw on was my experience. I am sure that, on some unconscious level, I was terrified during our wedding journey. Going from zero relatives to a few dozen in eight minutes flat was a little scary, especially when, for me, relatives equaled trauma. It's been quite an amazing transition.

Holly and Rob had lived with each other for five years and shared two children. Yet, when they decided to marry, as Rob told us, "Suddenly we found ourselves examining aspects of our relationship — with each other, with our kids, and even with our families. And we realized that we needed to change in many areas in order to fit our ideas of what we wanted from a formal marriage."

How has your engagement launched you into a new way of life, a new way of viewing yourselves? If you haven't thought about it, spend time over dinner, take a walk, or make a special date to discuss the changes you're experiencing. Talk about how deepening the bond you share influences you for the better. Notice that you are strengthened to speak up for yourselves or that you're learning to laugh and joke when you take yourselves too seriously or that you are sharing and encouraging each other to take risks that will make your wedding truly special.

By living out your commitment as a couple throughout the planning process, you will experience new possibilities and new levels of awareness. That is precisely the purpose and result of a true initiation.

The Value of Reality

The atmosphere surrounding the traditional wedding, right from the engagement onward, is typically steeped in fantasy. He is her knight in shining armor. She is a princess. With the bride and her mother arranging everything and her parents footing the bill, all too often money is no object, even in families that can hardly afford expensive weddings. The details, from the never-ending guest list to the seating arrangement for the reception, take on momentous importance, casting a burdensome shadow over what is supposed to be a joyously sacred time. And, once the special day is over, friends, marriage counselors, therapists, and the clergy are left to handle the shock of unmet expectations and the heartache of fantasies unfulfilled.

It is very important to the success of your wedding and your married life that you both remain grounded in the reality of your circumstances. By doing so, you'll affirm your acceptance of who you are, whether you're wealthy or of modest means, and that acceptance is a sign of self-love. You won't reject yourselves or try to become someone you're not. You are free to tell the truth of who you are, as that truth is the basis of real romance — a romance you can trust, a romance that will grow with you throughout your life together.

This doesn't mean that you are stuck in your current circumstances. It means that you are building your life on a foundation of honesty, integrity, self-regard, confidence, and character. As you grow and change, so will your circumstances, and, as they do, you can appreciate and express them with the same openness and sincerity. To focus on and trust in the reality of your relationship is a sign that you have the emotional, intellectual, and spiritual maturity you need to make your marriage a success.

When Paige and JC Keeler were married, her father had the means to give her as glamorous a wedding as she wanted. And he did. (Later in the book, Paige describes just what their wedding was like in chapter 14.) However, no matter what they could afford, their relationship and, as a result, their wedding were grounded in an appreciation of what they meant to each other, a connection that was simple and down to earth. Paige said:

One of my favorite memories from the wedding was something that we shared about ourselves with the group. For an appetizer at our formal wedding dinner, we chose individual chicken potpies. JC and I stood to explain to everyone why chicken potpies were on the menu.

Before JC and I started dating, we were very good friends. And at one point we were discussing relationships and sharing our relationship woes, as friends often do. JC said he was holding out for his "chicken potpie girl." When I inquired what that meant, he told me that he was looking for someone who would make a chicken potpie dinner in front of a rented movie as special an occasion as a fancy dinner and theater tickets. He meant that he was waiting for the real thing.

A year went by before we started dating. One night, after we had been seeing each other for about two months, we were out for a walk and JC told me that he had found her. When I asked who he'd found, he told me he'd found his chicken potpie girl and that I was that person. I had totally forgotten about the conversation until that night. Needless to say, I was floored.

Another year went by and we were engaged, and then another year [passed] before we were married. We often talked about having our first chicken potpie date but never got around to it. So, as we were planning the wedding, we decided that we would make the first course of the reception dinner our first official chicken potpie date and that everyone there who meant so much to us would share in something so dear. We told our guests, "Every time we eat chicken potpie in the future, we will think of you and this special night."

Since the wedding we've had many chicken potpie dates, and we always spend the time talking about the wedding. We also enjoy the emails we receive from people after they have had chicken potpie, letting us know that they were thinking of us and our wedding.

Paige and JC were devoted to the truth of who they are as people. Yes, their wedding was glamorous. But the chicken potpies — simple, earthy, and real — proved to be one of the most memorable moments for them and for their guests. Why? Because they had the power of being real.

When You Can't Do It Together

Sometimes, no matter how much the two of you want to be equal partners in your wedding planning, one of you simply isn't available. Yet, as the following story proves, if your hearts are joined, neither of you will be left out.

When Nissa Weaver married Major Stephen Van Riper, USMC, she had to be the prime mover in preparing their military-style wedding on the beach in Coronado, California:

Nine months before our wedding, after having just returned from eleven months of deployment himself, Steve became the director of Division Schools at Camp Pendleton, California. He was now in charge of training the instructors who would train the second wave of marines deploying to Iraq. It was a high-stress position with long hours, which didn't leave us much time for each other, let alone for him to help with planning the wedding.

He asked for only two things: to wear his blues, and to have veto power over everything else (meaning he let me have carte blanche unless he really just couldn't live with something). By the way, I would have been content to let him plan the entire wedding had my job been the more demanding of the two.

Since so many of Steve's friends were deployed to Iraq and other places around the world and couldn't come to the wedding, many of the wives attended alone or with their young children. To make sure no one was left out, Steve's sister made a big sign that said "Semper Fi" (*semper fidelis*, "always faithful," is the motto of the United States Marine Corps) and also a bunch of individual signs, each with a deployed marine's name on it. Then Steve and I gathered with all the marines who were at the wedding and had the photographer take a picture of the group. Each one of us held a sign saying, "Semper Fi, Andy," "Semper Fi, Dave," and so on so that they would know that we were holding them close in our hearts. Our photographer emailed those pictures to me immediately after the wedding, at no charge, to distribute to their wives.

The Magic of Your Differences

You no doubt have differing points of view about your wedding. Sometimes it might seem that it would be easier to design your wedding alone. But what would that say about your readiness to share a home, a family, and all the myriad choices you'll have to make together all along the way?

An easy way out is to opt for conformity, for being told what to do, for doing it like everyone else has done it so many times before. But that choice prohibits the vitality a successful marriage requires: a marriage thrives on moments of new awareness, awareness that creates change, and change that keeps love alive and growing.

A true marriage of two hearts, minds, bodies, and souls always results in transformation. When you view your wedding as an opportunity to discover and express your individual as well as your shared creativity, you'll be changed by your differences and the means you develop to resolve them when they clash. You are joined together and transformed by your dedication to the love that lives between you. That transformation, more than the ceremony itself, is your actual wedding.

Laura Danon sent us a short remembrance of how she was influenced by the differences between herself and her husband, Chas:

Chas and I were looking at the grounds of a lovely hotel, and I became more and more frustrated that we weren't making a decision.

"We have three months to find the perfect spot for our ceremony," I wailed, tears streaming down my face. "I've never been married before and I want everything to be perfect. Where are you?"

"Over here," Chas said. He was crouched down, staring at a beautiful orange-and-black butterfly. "Look at these wings. Have you ever seen anything more beautiful?"

"No," I said. "Now can you please get focused? We could stand here, with the sun setting behind us, or maybe over there on the grass."

"Wow, this would be great for my collection," he continued, ignoring my urgings to get on with the plans for the wedding. "I don't have a net. I'll just have to memorize its beauty."

The wedding was supposed to be outside. It rained. We hadn't planned for that. Spontaneously we made other arrangements, and it was a perfect day.

Twenty years later, and three years past his death, what lives on in my heart is the memory of a man so present to the moment that he did not want to lose a second of joy or the beauty of a passing butterfly.

A Wedding That Celebrates Who You Are

Uniqueness and individuality are at the heart of what we call real-life love. Instead of being pigeonholed into a stereotype, wouldn't you rather be loved for who you really are and supported in maintaining your sense of self, distinct from your partner, while blending together as a couple?

Your wedding journey offers you the opportunity to do just that, to appreciate the magic of your differences inspiring rich understanding and deep discovery of what is true and real about each of you. As you make ready to join together in marriage, you can empower yourselves, individually and as a couple, to plan your wedding so that your special day will be relaxed and laced with love and you will be prepared to embrace all that marriage has to offer.

By following our chapter-by-chapter guidelines for letting your love lead, you can make your wedding a joyous, one-of-a-kind, spiritually enriched and enriching event. The differences between you and your partner will become a genuinely romantic expression of your identity as a couple, and you will enjoy the wedding of your dreams.

CHAPTER 2

Popping the Questions

I met Lore in Germany during a business trip. Our courtship was largely by phone and email. But for her thirtieth birthday I arrived at her parents' home in Munich wearing a Trachtenanzug *[German suit]. And then during a private moment I proposed to her in German, asking, "Willst du mich heiraten?" She started to say, "Ja," but then said, "Yes, oh yes!" We married each other and our two different cultures.*

— Al Burton, dentist, New Jersey

Your engagement is your declaration to yourselves that your lives as single people have come to an end and your married life has begun. No matter how long you've been together or what promises you might have made to each other, your engagement is your first formal vow. And it sets the stage for all that is yet to come.

There are few moments in life that are truly transformational, moments in which you become someone you were not before. Becoming engaged is one of those moments.

We admire Al's sensitivity to Lore's German roots. He not

17

only asked her to marry him but also made it clear that he was embracing her culture. Because he asked in her own language, his proposal was deeply romantic and equally intimate. Lore needed no further proof that Al loved her for all that she was — and what could be better than that?

When the two of you join in your willingness to marry, your decision taps deeply into the awesome well of mysteries that spawns new life. You answer the call of one of the most profound human longings — the desire for loving connection between a man and a woman. No wonder the words *engagement, wedding,* and *honeymoon* bring a smile to the lips, warmth to the heart, and a flood of dazzling expectations of how things will be.

There is no template for the engagement moment. Regardless of what you've already done or are planning to do — and regardless of whether your dreams are strictly traditional, ultramodern, or quirky — from the moment you say, "Yes, we will," your engagement will forever carry its own unique stamp.

Melanie and Brian met online and, after a while, moved in together. After he knew that he would propose, he searched for the ring online, chose the stones — diamonds and sapphires — online, had them appraised online by a gemologist in another state, selected the design online, and had the ring built through an online source. He did not actually see it until two days before he proposed.

The day of the big question went off almost flawlessly. He took their dog, Jake, out to the park for his morning romp, came home, and made coffee. Next he strung a length of blue ribbon through the ring and tied it to Jake's collar. With coffee on a tray, he entered the bedroom to wake Melanie. The only hitch was Jake's timing. He didn't wait for Brian's command. Instead, expressing his own excitement, Jake leapt up on the bed with

the ring dangling from his neck. There was no way Melanie could miss it. At that point, Brian knelt by the side of the bed and proposed.

There they were. Jake barking. Melanie teary. And Brian very, very proud.

Capturing Love

Today a man hopes to capture a woman's heart, to have her love him in return. But that wasn't always the case. In fact, in ancient times, when people lived in small villages with strict taboos against inbreeding, marriage by capture was the strategy of the husband-on-the-hunt.

A man and his best friend — his "best man" — would raid a nearby village to steal the woman he wanted. If he was able to keep his bride from fleeing, she was legally his for life. To prevent her escape, he made a cord of grasses to tie her hands and feet. After she resigned herself to her new situation and he felt sure that she would stay, he released her. Then he tied a braided ring around her finger to symbolize her status as his possession. He had tied the knot — literally.

Engagements are far different today, of course. If you're already engaged, your proposal might or might not have been something you did equally and together. But if you are still considering how to go about it, wouldn't it be better, wiser, and far more intimate to begin by engaging in discussions that cover the essential issues each successful married couple must come to terms with? And even if you are already engaged, many more questions remain to be answered beyond "Will you marry me?" We call this "popping the questions," and we advise all couples to address The Ten Key Issues of Married Life long before they get married.

The Ten Key Issues of Married Life

The intimacy of your marriage, which actually began developing at the moment you first met, stems from your openness, your willingness to reveal yourselves, and your growth into an understanding and acceptance of who you really are. You can become intimate in all kinds of ways: by having fun; by being quiet; by facing and resolving conflicts; and by discussing your beliefs, your desires and needs, and your vision of married life with each other.

While it might seem that selecting your invitations is the most pressing issue of the day, we remind you that you are planning your entire future, not just a onetime ceremony. That is why playing the romantic "game" of popping the questions is essential before you can truly take charge of your life together and demonstrate your authority as an adult couple throughout the remaining months of wedding preparation.

Your answers to the following questions will create the foundation for your future partnership. Therefore, no matter how close you are to your wedding date, we strongly advise you to make time for these questions. Take turns answering each question aloud. Then, topic by topic, discuss any feelings, issues, and especially disagreements that emerge.

To fully gauge where each of you stands, you might want to set aside a separate time to address each topic. As you explore your thoughts and feelings on each of these issues, a picture of your expectations and imaginings of married life will emerge — and magic will happen as you find ways to combine what you both want into a future that you hadn't even imagined before these talks.

You don't have to take these questions in the order we list them. Start with whatever feels most comfortable, and don't hesitate to add new topics inspired by what you share with each other.

Spending Habits and Financial Objectives

❖ *How do you feel about money?*

❖ *Is having a lot of money essential to you?*

❖ *Are you more of a spender or a saver? Why?*

❖ *How do you feel about creating budgets and sticking to them?*

❖ *What is your experience with saving and investing money?*

❖ *Who will keep the books for your family's accounts?*

❖ *What are your financial goals for one year from now? Five years? Ten years?*

Religion/Spiritual Practice

❖ *What do you believe about God?*

❖ *Do you practice a particular religion or spiritual discipline?*

❖ *If so, what does it require of you? What is important to you about it?*

❖ *In what, if any, religion will you want to raise the children you might have?*

❖ *Do you believe in an afterlife? In a life before this life?*

❖ *What are your religious/spiritual goals?*

Parents and In-Laws

❖ *Which family will you view as central: your families of origin or the family you are creating together?*

❖ *How often will you want to visit your parents and/or have them visit you?*

❖ *How often will you want to have phone conversations with your parents?*

❖ *If your parents live nearby, will you want them to feel free to drop by at any time?*

❖ *How will you deal with your families about who goes where on what holiday?*

❖ *If conflict arises, are you prepared to defend your marriage against intrusions by your parents and/or other relatives?*

Children

❖ *Do you want children? If yes, why? If not, why not? (Skip to the next topic if you both answer no.)*

❖ *How many children do you want? Why?*

❖ *How will you support them financially?*

❖ *When do you imagine you will have them?*

❖ *Will one of you work while the other stays at home with the children? Or will you leave the children at a day-care center or with a relative or nanny?*

❖ *What do you consider to be proper discipline?*

Socializing and Friends

❖ *Do you prefer stay-at-home activities such as reading, watching television, or using the computer? Or do you prefer to go out with friends, play sports, go dancing, and so on?*

❖ *How important are your friends?*

❖ *How much time do you expect to spend with your friends and away from your spouse?*

❖ *Can you call on your friends if you need help, and vice versa?*

❖ *If necessary, would you choose your spouse and family over your friends?*

Career Goals

❖ *What do you most want to be doing in ten to twenty years?*

❖ *What level of status and income do you expect?*

❖ *What education or special training is required for you to attain your goal?*

❖ *How do your career goals coincide or conflict with your partner's?*

❖ *What adjustments would you make in order to satisfy yourself and your partner?*

❖ *Do you feel supportive of your partner's career aspirations?*

❖ *Do you wish you or your partner were more ambitious? Less ambitious? Why?*

❖ *How might your/your partner's career goals affect your children?*

Sex

❖ *How important is sex to your happiness?*

❖ *How satisfied are you with your sex life?*

❖ *What changes do you want in frequency or activity?*

❖ *If illness or other factors were to make sex impossible,
what problems, if any, would you have?*

❖ *Are you prepared to focus differently on your sexual
relationship when the thrill and excitement of newness
wear off and you might need to learn new ways to
become aroused?*

❖ *Do you expect to find your partner sexually attractive
when you are in your older years?*

Self-Development

❖ *Do you have an interest in learning more about yourself
or the world?*

❖ *How important is it for you to attend classes and lectures
or go to cultural events?*

❖ *Do you read to educate yourself or just to relax and have fun?*

❖ *Would you be willing to go to counseling if you needed
personal or relationship help? If no, why not?*

❖ *How important is it for you both to be committed to
personal development?*

❖ *How do you think your/your spouse's personal development
will affect your marriage?*

Health/Appearance/Physical Fitness

❖ *How important is your/your spouse's physical appearance?*

❖ *How important is your/your spouse's diet and weight?*

❖ *Do you worry about health issues?*

❖ *Do you expect to maintain a regular exercise regime after
you're married? After you've had children?*

❖ *Is it important that you exercise together or alone? Why?*

❖ *Do you prefer traditional medical care or alternative/preventative medicine?*

Bad Habits

❖ *Do you have any bad habits that could affect your marriage over the long term?*

❖ *Does your partner have any bad habits that could affect you if they weren't altered?*

❖ *How open are you to constructive criticism from your partner?*

❖ *How open are you to offering constructive criticism?*

❖ *How open are you to making a sincere effort to change your habits?*

❖ *Are there any make-or-break issues your partner should know about?*

As you can see, popping these questions provides you with a strong basis of understanding and establishes a shared foundation for your marriage. And while your choice of wine or bridal veil might be uppermost on your mind right now, your confidence in all your wedding selections will be greatly enhanced once you've enlarged and grounded your love by thoroughly answering these questions. When you allow love to lead and offer self-revealing disclosures to your partner, your decision to marry will be supported by genuinely intimate, truly romantic and loving knowledge of each other.

Remember, just as foreplay opens the way for sex, your engagement foreshadows your marriage. Therefore, the more you protect your love, your relationship, and your future happiness by becoming engaged in self-awareness and understanding, the more trustworthy and meaningful it will be when you actually say "I do" during your final vows.

The Proposal

For those of you who are not yet engaged, we strongly advise you to pop all the questions above before you officially agree to marry. That way, your basis for proposing and saying yes will be profoundly meaningful and secure.

Of course, the style in which you officially propose is strictly up to you and your shared idea of fun and romance. Here are two wonderfully fun and romantic examples.

Pauline Lambert and Jerrod O'Neil worked in the same high-rise in Chicago for more than three years. But they may never have met if they hadn't been riding the same elevator when it got stuck on the eleventh floor. Although there were four people sharing their plight, the time it took to free them seemed to fly as Pauline and Jerrod exchanged casual conversation. Later Jerrod sent Pauline eleven carnations and called to ask her out.

They soon discovered that Pauline was born on the eleventh of May, and Jerrod on the eleventh of July. And they still talk about how it gave them shivers to see how the magical number eleven was playing out in their lives.

Several months later, Jerrod chose the perfect place for his proposal — the Signature Room restaurant atop the John Hancock building. But then he had a better idea. Making sure they were alone during the ninety-five-floor elevator ride up to the restaurant, Jerrod said, "I couldn't think of a better place to ask if you'll marry me." Pauline's squeal of delight echoed throughout the restaurant as the doors opened. Nearly a year later they were married on November eleventh with matching wedding bands each set with eleven diamonds.

Brad and Maren both enjoyed playing softball on their church team. In fact, that's how they realized they were attracted to each other, lingering after practice to chat, and then eventually making it a habit to go for pizza. Soon they knew they were seriously in love and ready for commitment.

One year after their first official date, Maren, never afraid to break tradition, gave Brad a bat engraved with, "I'll go to bat for you anytime. Let's get married. Your greatest fan, Maren."

Nearly in tears, Brad was thrilled. "You landed a home run with that one, you sweetheart! How soon can we arrange the wedding?"

While becoming formally committed is thrilling, we encourage you to keep the excitement to yourselves for a short while. Allow your bond to grow deeper and your determination to marry on your own terms to ripen. When you are ready to break the news, remember that you are grown-ups. Make sure your bond isn't invaded by those who will assure you that they know best what will make your wedding perfect.

The Question of Your Rings

That engagement, wedding, and even anniversary rings are set with diamonds is now taken for granted. But the fact is that in the late nineteenth century, De Beers, a mining and distribution company, discovered large diamond mines in South Africa. Tiffany's followed by designing the diamond solitaire. These two events sparked a marketing revolution that assured the popularity of the diamond engagement ring among the general public. It is to De Beers that we owe the famous slogan "A Diamond Is Forever."

Today couples can consider all sorts of rings. There are bridal sets in which the engagement ring and wedding band lock together or intertwine; his-and-hers matching wedding bands;

and diamond rings intended for anniversaries. If you haven't already selected your rings, you might want to think ahead. For example, you might want to later add a "past, present, and future" ring (with three stones), an anniversary band (with a row of diamonds), or an "eternity" ring (with diamonds all around the band).

If you cannot find a ring to your liking, or you want to have an heirloom that belonged to one of your grandmothers reset or redesigned, you can consult with an independent jewelry designer such as Bridget Gless (www.bridgetglessdesigns.com).

Bridget told us, "Many couples have a very clear idea of what they want, but don't know who to turn to for help. Some jewelry stores offer design services and jewelry designers can be found in the yellow pages and online. Allow the designer to teach you about the quality of stones so that you know what you are getting. Most important, when you have a one-of-a-kind ring created, request to see the mold before the ring is cast."

After we became engaged, we couldn't find a ring we liked, so we had a jeweler in the Los Angeles Jewelry Mart design what we consider *our* engagement ring, which Judith wears. A pear-shaped solitaire is encircled by small baguettes that reach outward like a starburst. Since we were both employed, we shared the cost of the ring, plus a gold tie tack for Jim's engagement jewelry, Judith's simple little gold wedding band, and Jim's gold wedding band, inlaid with four white diamonds. They were our joint investment in the future.

When Aaron decided to propose to Sondra, he took the risk of first selecting the ring, a simple gold band inlaid with eight diamonds — yellow, blue, white, and green. "I would have waited until Valentine's Day, but Sondra, a professional snowboarder, had a commitment that prevented us from being together on that day," Aaron said. So, two days before Valentine's

Day, as they were perched on the top of Mount Baldy in Sun Valley, Idaho, ready to take off down the slope, Aaron proposed.

Not only did she love the ring, she was stunned by the magic of it. Just a few weeks earlier, when a woman had oohed and aahed that a certain cut of diamond was so "in," Sondra had said that all she wanted was "a simple band inlaid with diamonds." However, she'd never told that to Aaron.

When the time came to think about a wedding ring, Sondra began to ask herself, "Do I need another ring?" The answer was a resounding *no*. Not because she didn't want Aaron to put out more money, but because she really didn't want another ring.

Aaron's own wedding band — white and yellow gold inlaid with one blue diamond — served as his engagement ring as well. "I started wearing it as soon as I got it — and never took it off," Aaron chuckled. "Since we trekked up to Machu Picchu for our wedding, I must have had the dirtiest ring anyone ever used in their wedding."

Heather told us that when she and Jim were discussing marriage, they agreed that they wanted to mutually decide upon the details of their wedding. Shopping together for her ring, they selected a topaz set with diamonds in a gold band; because those are their birthstones, their choice was unique to them and far more personally meaningful than a typical solitaire.

Yet, although Heather and Jim loved the process of shopping for the ring, when she told her friends, most were scandalized. Why would she want anything but for her man to buy the ring and surprise her when he proposed? Furthermore, her friends insisted that shopping together destroyed the romance. But because Heather and Jim shopped and paid for their ring together, they discovered a depth of intimacy and romance they hadn't anticipated.

In addition to their personalized and independent approach,

Heather still wanted the delight of being surprised when Jim formally proposed and gave her the ring. He obliged by setting up an elaborate ruse, and she was enchanted.

Of course, you might not want diamonds at all. You might not even want an engagement ring. Whatever your taste and decision, and no matter what anyone else has done, follow only what is right for you.

Ready but Not Wealthy

Smart couples think more than twice before going into debt to buy their rings. Why? Because it's less than romantic to begin your married life by living beyond your means and burdening your love with financial problems.

Yet the choice of the engagement ring is fraught with serious anxiety for some women and the men who love them. As a client told us, "I can trust that Ginny will like whatever I buy as long as it's bigger than what her friends have."

We strongly suggest that you avoid bowing down to the lord of the ring offering your financial burden as a sacrifice to what is actually a stereotype of love and romance. Love is nothing if it is not real. So, when the two of you choose a ring that you can reasonably afford, that ring will take on added value. It will symbolize your recognition, respect, and appreciation of the very real, down-to-earth decision you have made. If you can afford something more later, the two of you can shop for a new gem, respectful of the mature love you've already practiced and earned.

Where's His Engagement Ring?

If you truly respect the decision you are making together, why should the bride be the only one to wear a sign of commitment?

Anyone who sees a woman's ring understands that she is spoken for. But traditionally, the groom doesn't wear a ring. Publicly, he still appears to be available.

As Marie said to us, "Why doesn't he wear an engagement ring? Isn't he taken?" When we asked if her fiancé had worn a ring, she told us, "He decided on his own to wear a simple silver band until we were married. And I enjoyed buying it for him."

In this time of equal opportunity, we are pleased to see engagement customs beginning to expand. More grooms are choosing to wear their own form of an engagement ring, whether it's a silver band, their wedding band, or something uniquely discovered or created by the couple.

United through Dialogue

When your wedding journey is guided by popping the questions, your confidence and deepening partnership will strengthen you against those who might want to invade your planning with intrusive questions and controlling demands. You'll be joined in your determination to marry only in a manner that expresses your own needs and desires.

United through your ongoing dialogue — sincere and open talking and, even more important, sincere and open listening — you will forge, during the time of your engagement, the foundation for the type of marriage you both desire. Through dialogue, the two of you will begin your shared life on a basis of real romance and mutual respect. And through dialogue, your understanding of each other and of what love means to each of you will continue to evolve as you grow and change, individually and together.

Now you have an engagement worthy of its name.

CHAPTER 3

Whose Wedding Is It, Anyway?

My fiancé was 100 percent involved with the planning and preparation for our wedding. We divvied up the tasks, talked through the disagreements we encountered, and mostly had fun. That relieved a lot of stress for me. And it made it our wedding instead of my wedding.

— Erica, police officer, New Jersey

*A*s a conscious man and woman, you have the opportunity to join together with emotional authority and financial maturity in the planning of your wedding. This is a break with tradition, but it is not only a welcome trend, it is gradually changing society's expectations of how weddings should be.

A New Trend

The wedding's move away from its old identity as a day produced by the bride's parents — and focused almost exclusively on her — to a new identity as a day that recognizes, respects, and esteems both the bride and the groom marks a profound spiritual leap from its historic roots, when fathers literally sold their daughters to grooms and receptions celebrated that legal exchange of property.

As more couples choose to be married in their own uniquely special ways, no longer is the groom left out of the planning and preparation. No longer does the wedding belong to the parents — whether just the parents of the bride or both sets of parents — who were in charge of their children's nuptials in the past (and, in some circles, still are today). But why would you want to be treated as children at your own wedding?

That's one of the reasons we are pleased to see the groom taking center stage along with the bride. Sharing the limelight will establish you as an adult couple who is truly ready for married life. And it makes for a great time together. If this idea is new to you, consider these words from new brides who wrote to usabride.com:

EDYTA: "The best thing about our wedding was that my husband and I did everything together — from addressing invitations to purchasing materials and making centerpieces, decorating the hall, and all other aspects of the wedding."

SHERI: "My husband voluntarily involved himself in every aspect of planning the wedding. He even helped me pick out my dress. It all made for a wonderfully fun experience!"

ALISON: "We felt free to do things our way. Remember that it's your wedding, not your mother's, sister's, or best friend's. Instead of a formal processional, we played

'Going to the Chapel' as I went down the aisle. People laughed and thought it was so much fun."

KEYA: "I myself am a wedding coordinator and had first-hand experience [in] planning every detail of my wedding. The highlight was having my husband plan our wedding with me. He had some great input — he even picked out my shoes."

Another bride, Janetta, a professional acquaintance of ours, said, "When Roberto and I started discussing what we wanted, it was obvious that we would need to collaborate every step of the way because we had such diverse opinions of what constituted the 'right' way." Then she added with a laugh, "Besides, neither one of us wanted to feel left out or bossed around by the other."

While you might decide to ask friends and relatives to participate, and they can be very helpful, keep in mind that they are *helping* you — both of you — not making decisions about what you *should* be doing.

A Rehearsal for Your Marriage

The beauty of creating your wedding together is that you'll make clear to all who know you that you are a seriously loving couple. You won't be just caught up in wedding fever or rushing to the altar to keep up with your friends. You will be consciously joined and establishing yourselves as ready for marriage.

Since a loving partnership can be achieved only when you're both invested in discovering what is best for your relationship, doesn't it make sense to practice working together now rather than waiting until after your marriage? Use this precious time to discover the friction points that could later upset your marriage, and learn how to resolve them to your mutual satisfaction. Indeed, by making all your decisions as a team, you'll encounter not only many delightful romantic surprises, but also some not-so-delightful shocks about your differences. Yet when you follow your commitment to love, you'll gain new insights and confidence in your relationship all along the way.

In rare instances, the planning process provides the couple with a "trouble ahead" warning, making it clear that they won't be able to make it in the long term. Unable to work out their conflicts about timing, taste, and/or other priorities, they have the opportunity to change their minds. They save themselves from an inevitable divorce when the same lack of respect and shared values grows to torturous proportions. Calling off their wedding is not only a giant relief; it is a real success, even though it might be painful and embarrassing in the short run.

In every other case — such as yours — you'll be reassured that you are a terrific team. A loving couple who shares responsibilities and communicates openly about your fears (marriage better come with some fears, or you're not taking it seriously) and challenges (such as staying within budget or whether to invite alcoholic Aunt Dora, who might spoil everything), you'll find that you are indeed well mated.

What about Your Parents?

"I became engaged five months ago, and I feel so alone. We keep putting off setting the date because, by doing it the way we want, it seems we'll hurt so many people who expect the old traditional way." That's what Julie Champagne, makeup artist for *More to Life*, TVOntario in Toronto, told us as we were waiting to do the show. We applauded Julie for her sensitivity to others, but we also encouraged her to join with her fiancé to strengthen their resolve to marry on their own terms.

While we are certainly sensitive to the disappointment some parents experience when their offspring "spring off" to go their own wedding way, we also must make the point that marriage is a commitment made by adults. Taking responsibility will not only establish you as a mature and capable couple in your community, but also will guard against dangerous, grandiose fantasies that could sweep you away if someone else does most of the work and foots the bill. And there's more to those fantasies than mere expense. They can trap you in an emotional bubble that will eventually burst. And nothing is as painful as a fantasy world blown apart by reality. Your wedding is very special, as is the process that leads up to it. Join together and serve your love. Love grows best when your feet are rooted in the reality of your relationship.

It's worth repeating that when you claim authority over your wedding, you'll reduce the likelihood of interference and intrusion by well-meaning friends and relatives who unconsciously believe they have the right to dictate what you should and should not do.

Sondra and Aaron spoke with us after they had returned from their wedding amid the ruins of Machu Picchu in Peru. She was astonished at how "the minute we announced we were engaged, everyone else seemed to think they knew what we should do." "Yeah," Aaron chimed in. "People couldn't wait to suggest ideas to me and plan the wedding. It was amazing."

Evelyn wrote to us just after her wedding: "In committing to my husband, I realized I was actively changing my own and other people's roles in the family and in my own social circle. It's amazing how people didn't like it and didn't even realize that this was upsetting them. Learning, accepting, and working through this new terrain — putting ourselves and each other first to establish our own family unit — were so essential to creating intimacy and success in our marriage. It wasn't necessarily easy, but it opened the door to immense trust and freedom in our relationship."

So, with compassion for the upsets that your parents and others close to you might experience, take responsibility for what you want. After all, once the big day has passed, it will be up to you, and only you, to build your life together. Why wait until then to start?

Your Dream Wedding

Despite the fact that weddings are meant for both the bride and groom, many women have dreamed about their "perfect" day since they were very young, not always including the groom in their imaginings. If this is the case for you, no doubt you and your mom take care of everything in that fantasy. You imagine that it will be *your* day and that it will go off without a hitch. Elegant. Romantic. Flawless.

We've spoken with a number of single women who've told us something like "Oh, I've always known what kind of wedding I'll have...the kind of ring he'll give me, how he'll propose, what gown I'll wear, even the flowers I'll carry." But the majority of these women weren't even dating, and not one was in a serious relationship. When we asked about the groom, their response was just as definitive: "Oh, he'll be fine with whatever I decide."

Renee was so in love with weddings that she still had her bride doll collection. She even had a couple of grooms in the collection, but it was the glamorous brides that inspired her to study fashion design. For Renee's wedding, her mother hired workers to build a three-tiered garden — complete with a grotto (which was filled with potted orchids for the affair) and a fountain. Her husband said, "It felt like we were props in a play."

Your dream of the perfect wedding is enchanting. We know that. But, as in Renee's case and in so many others, your awesome dream and your mother's dream can sneak up and take over, and, before you know it, you've got a grotto in the backyard.

Ideas of the dream wedding keep changing, and some elements of today's "perfect" wedding were unheard of just twenty-five years ago. Nevertheless, the idea that the wedding day is *her* day, the day for her to feel like a princess, remains deep and pervasive in our culture.

However, as marriage counselors for many years, we've witnessed numerous times how a gulf was created right from the beginning when the bride assumed that the groom would not be involved — either because she thought he wouldn't care or because her mother took over and ran the show (and that's what the wedding often turned out to be, a show). So we urge you to consciously and thoughtfully make certain that your wedding — from the engagement all the way through the honeymoon — represents you and your husband, not you and your dream, or you and your mom's dream, or, perhaps, even *just* your mom's dream.

It's a wedding for you and your groom. It's your marriage and your life. Don't lose sight of that fact.

A New Dream

It's not our intent to take away your dream. If you're dreaming of a certain wedding gown that makes you look spectacular and that you can afford within the budget the two of you have set, we strongly encourage you to buy it. But if the dress costs far more than you can reasonably afford, you, as an adult embarking on a new way of life, would be wise to stay alert and examine your priorities. Discuss the issue with your fiancé. Maybe you'll want to shop together to find an entirely different kind of gown that fits your budget and your dreams of beauty but still allows you to keep your financial responsibility, emotional integrity, and loving relationship as your central focus.

If you are truly dedicated to fulfilling your dream, yet want to protect your relationship from wedding fever, the most important step you can take is to involve your groom in everything. Talk with him. Explain why your wedding just won't feel like *yours* if it's not how you've always imagined. Fill him in on all the details.

However you proceed, remain conscious that your husband-to-be is your partner and should never be excluded from your wedding plans. He is an adult in his own right, an equal to you, and he should be part of the process.

It is our hope that you will move toward a new vision co-created by the two of you. The vision you build together will be far richer and more meaningful than your private fantasies. After all, marital success will depend in part on your ability to abandon fantasies about marriage, about how your husband should be, and even about how you should behave as a wife. Only then can you give yourself fully to the truth of your actual life together.

The Groom

Modern Bride magazine (August/September 2002) published a tuxedo advertisement that made clear that the groom's role, as it's conventionally understood, is essentially inconsequential. The ad quotes a groom as saying, "Everyone knows weddings are for the bride. I'm simply an accessory with (hopefully) some fringe benefits in years to come. Being an accessory, though, it's crucial that I look my very best for her wedding. It's pretty likely I'll embarrass her at some point, but I sure don't want it to be on her wedding day."

That idea is, of course, not new. A 1929 edition of *Vogue's Book of Brides* states that if a bride wants to "realize her youthful dreams regarding her wedding [and] if the young couple and the bride's family are willing — though perhaps we should say that the groom is *resigned* rather than willing — there is no reason why such tastes should not be indulged" (italics ours).

Is it any wonder that, in the past, men have struggled to feel important in their marriage relationships? They've been all but sidelined on the path to the altar, and their desire to marry at all has been dampened by the idea that they are simply resigned accessories. No doubt this traditional exclusion of grooms has helped to set the stage for their later lack of participation in marriage.

Yet, according to a survey of more than three thousand women conducted by *Bride's* magazine and reported in its summer 2003 issue, today's men aren't willing to be just resigned accessories. "In their 20s, 6 out of 10 couples (61 percent) are shouldering the tasks together. That figure jumps to 76 percent for twosomes in their 30s, and 88 percent for duos in their 40s." Clearly the vast majority of today's grooms actively participate in planning the transitional rites through which they will leave singlehood and become husbands.

While such participation will certainly increase marital success and satisfaction, some men still raise concerns. One groom, Harv, went as far as to express his dissatisfaction with the disparity between how brides and grooms look on the day of their weddings. "Women are expected to be (and want to be) glamorous and beautiful. And to make them more so, the men are expected to look like penguins. . . . I suggest new, courageous, fancy, and fun attire for men, ceremonial dress that shows off male beauty in all the wonder it is."

Larry told us that if he could do his wedding over, having "resigned my role to showing up at the church on time, . . . I would opt for a do-it-yourself affair." Why? Because his bride's father was hostile to him throughout the process, as though his daughter were still his little girl and Larry an interloper. He remembers "feeling guilty that my in-laws got stuck with a big price tag. . . . It occurred to me that part of the reason that I felt bad about the money is that I felt emasculated and incompetent, boyish even."

Open to Being Changed

All too often, planning is associated with control — the bride's predetermined ideas, which must be executed no matter what; parental control of all kinds; and even the bride's and groom's attempts to control each other.

And that's why wedding planning has such a bad rap, as if it, too, were all about control. But control itself is not necessary. What *is* necessary, when you find yourself slipping out of control, is to open yourself to see the larger picture of the wedding process. When you find yourself becoming controlling, take a moment to ask yourself how this or that detail suddenly became more important than the joyous spirit of your coming marriage. If you feel consumed by perfectionism or worry-wart behavior, there might be old concerns you need to leave behind to ensure you won't be frazzled and frustrated on your special day. Now's the time to start practicing a more loving, spiritual acceptance of all that you are going through.

When you trust yourselves and stay open to each other's influence, you will be taken beyond who and how you've known yourselves to be. To achieve this transcendence, surrender your old expectations of how your relationship *should* be and how your wedding *should* be. Remember, love is a powerful guide and teacher. On the other side of *should*, you'll discover that delight — delicious, wondrous delight — awaits you in the mystery of your joining together.

Mark emailed us to explain how, some years ago, when he'd just been commissioned in the marines, he worked part-time while his soon-to-be-wife, Gloria, worked full-time. Since he had more free time, he did most of the running around and arranging for their wedding, going as far as to search out the particular fabric Gloria wanted for her gown. Out of true respect for flexibility and differing preferences, Gloria and Mark continued to step beyond stereotypical choices after their wedding. She is now the full-time breadwinner, while Mark is the stay-at-home dad and homemaker. Their open-hearted wedding adventure inadvertently helped them to discover the arrangement that best serves them in their marriage.

Phila and Erick Hoopes discovered a special sidelight on their wedding journey. During the last six months of their engagement, they spent a lot of time in his second-floor townhouse apartment, where the landlord had his photographic studio directly above them. Around winter solstice, they had a near make-or-break argument. They weren't asking for better treatment from each other, nor were they complaining about some emotional injury; rather, they each insisted that the other deserved better. As Phila told us:

At midnight, right at the point when it looked like the relationship was over, two Canada geese flew directly over the house, so low that we could hear their wings. As a rule, Canada geese don't fly at night, nor do they fly anywhere near Baltimore City in the winter. The windows were closed, so we shouldn't have been able to hear their wing strokes from the apartment since the landlord's studio, which had a twelve-foot ceiling, was upstairs.

We had just read a very powerful spiritual book about a couple who took geese as a symbol for their faithfulness. So it seemed at that moment as if the geese were a sign, as if Someone was trying to tell us something. Consequently, our fight had a very different ending than we had imagined just moments before. In fact, being together took on a much larger dimension, for it now seemed to both of us that our relationship held a place of destiny in our lives.

We designed our wedding rings with geese. I designed our Quaker wedding certificate with geese. And, amazing as it might sound, at each stop on our honeymoon, sometime during each day either live Canada geese would show up or we would come across an image of them. We saw them on the river, we discovered a painting of geese above our bed, and one time a fierce gaggle of geese surrounded us at a picnic table, demanding food.

Those particular geese were special. Without them, Phila would never have had to scramble to the top of the table while Erick protectively chased the geese away, giving her an opportunity to learn more about deserving and receiving his love.

Wedding Partners

When you, as a couple, keep the well-being of your relationship as your central guiding light throughout your wedding journey, yours will be a spiritually sacred commitment and celebration. Your awareness and dedication to that guiding light makes it unimaginable for only one of you to plan and produce your wedding without the other's involvement.

In order to get started or prompt new ideas, take turns sharing about the best weddings you've ever attended. Tell each other what made them so touching, so beautiful, and so memorable. Talk about how you want your guests to remember your own celebration, and what you want to show your children in your video years from now.

Make dates to visit florists, wedding and reception sites, caterers, DJs, party rental stores, tux and gown shops, and bridal fairs — any place that might trigger new ideas. Ask your friends for referrals beforehand and then go shopping together. Don't pin yourselves down on this first pass. These should be romantic "let's pretend" dates, so don't buy anything or place any orders. Taste things. Try things on. Ask lots and lots of questions. Take brochures, cards, and price lists. And, on your way out, be sure to say something such as "Thank you so much for your help. We are just beginning to look around." That way, you'll be free of any obligation and these outings will be smart fact-finding missions as well as enterprising and fun dates. Later, after you've crystallized your ideas you can readily return to vendors who impressed you, treated you with care and respect, and enjoyed exchanging ideas with you.

For us, the whole planning process was a terrific adventure. Because we had no preset ideas about what we wanted — except that we would do it together — everywhere we went offered fun and romantic possibilities. Our elegant toasting glasses came from a stroll through Geary's in Beverly Hills. We discovered our down-and-dirty rock 'n' roll blues band while dancing in a dive on the Santa Monica Pier.

As many couples have already discovered, weddings are far more meaningful, fulfilling, and personally empowering when both the bride and the groom are full partners in the cocreation of (and even payment for) their special day — a day they're able to enjoy and to look back on through shared, joy-filled memories for the rest of their lives.

CHAPTER 4

⋙

In Love or in Debt?

We got carried away. And it's all the little things that really add up! Now that it's over and we can barely pay our bills, it's clear we should have stuck to our original budget.

— Margo and Preston, landscape architects, Florida

Who pays and how much to pay for the wedding are central issues for the modern couple. While couples are increasingly choosing to pay some or all of the costs, the amount spent keeps climbing at an alarming rate.

Skyrocketing Price Tags

Again and again, our survey respondents expressed concern about the heavy financial burden today's typical wedding places on parents and/or the new couple. In the United States, the average wedding costs $27,000, and that often doesn't include the rings, the gown, or the honeymoon. Some brides, neither wealthy nor famous, spend more than that on their gowns alone. Friends rush to outdo friends, competing over the number of attendants, the type of decorations, the menus — every detail of these elaborate productions.

Why are so many couples more interested in splurging on a one-day megathon than in starting married life free of debt and with, perhaps, the down payment for a house? Or several thousand in mutual funds? Or a college fund started for their yet-to-be-born child?

When you focus on the spiritual importance of your wedding and on having your community witness your vows rather than on an extravagant production, you will be better able to maintain perspective on your own sincere values. There's no need to fall for ideas that seem fun or glamorous in the moment but, in retrospect, will disappoint you because they have no lasting value that warrants their expense.

Who Pays?

Historically, the bride's parents paid for everything. Then, as rehearsal for the ceremony became popular, the groom's parents took charge of paying for the rehearsal dinner. Still more recently, the rules of etiquette — once dictating that only the bride's parents should foot the bill for the wedding and reception — have relaxed, and now both sets of parents often share the cost.

But what psychological impact does parental payment (often for everything) have on the man and woman? Certainly, in some cases, the result is beautiful: the lovers feel embraced and cherished by their parents. But this arrangement leaves far too many couples entangled in their parents' purse strings. It can infringe on their creative style, suffocate their independence, and create tension, hostilities, and hurt feelings between the generations. As Liz told us, "It felt like it was my mother's wedding, the wedding she'd never had, not mine."

That's why it's a smart practice to pay for your wedding yourselves. When you do, you'll be free of emotional obligation, coercion, and any other loss of adult power and authority. More important, you'll affirm your ability to be financially responsible — which is certainly a key element in any successful marriage.

Planning and paying for your wedding offer the opportunity for both of you to demonstrate to yourselves and everyone who cares about the success of your marriage that you are indeed able to design, budget, organize, and follow through on your plans. You not only work together; you're also able to harmonize your financial differences into a rich symphony of creativity that makes your wedding an expression unique to the two of you.

If you are comfortable accepting financial help, that's fine. But be as responsible with your parents' funds as you would be with your own. Just like the bridal magazines, we advise you to consider cost-cutting possibilities, from holding your wedding ceremony and reception during the day (because brunch or lunch are less expensive than dinner) to borrowing anything you can from friends and family members who recently walked down the aisle (whether it's a tiara, jewelry, handbag, tuxedo, shoes, or whatever else you need).

But we're going even a step beyond that. Your wedding is not about how much you spend. It's about your own sense of style, why getting married is important and meaningful to you, what you know and cherish about each other, and what you want your guests to see, hear, and feel. Your wedding is about you, your character, your combined sensibilities, and your mutual vision of what being a couple means. These elements will give your wedding a mark of its own and make it memorable.

So, how might you create a perfect event while also staying within the limits of your current financial situation?

Bob and Elana's story offers a few ideas. A few years ago, even though Bob still had two more years of surgery residency to go, he decided to propose to Elana, who was then an elementary school teacher. Although they could barely afford their rent, they wanted to be married.

Elana's parents offered to give them a lavish wedding, but they declined, wanting to stay true to the reality of their circumstances. Bob came up with the solution, which turned out to be more memorable and joyous than they'd even imagined. And it cost them almost nothing.

Elana taught at a private school where teachers stayed with their classes for two years. Elana loved her fourth graders, whom she'd been with for more than a year, and they felt the same way about her. Bob and Elana met with her school principal to ask permission to hold their ceremony during the last hour of Elana's class on the day before Christmas vacation. It would be a gift from Elana to her class, and certainly their presence would be a gift to her and Bob. And, as they said, it would be a wonderful life experience for the kids.

The principal was delighted with the idea, given three conditions: that the event be a surprise so the children wouldn't be distracted with excitement throughout the day; that Elana prepare a social studies lesson on the wedding practices of various cultures to create a context for the wedding; and that she show her students pictures of Bob so that they wouldn't be frightened when he arrived. Elana agreed, and permission was granted.

Bob and Elana invited only family, very close friends, and, of course, the principal. Bob's uncle, a minister, officiated.

At the appointed hour, Bob swept through the door, picked Elana up, swung her around, and announced to the students, "Get ready. It's a wedding! I'm going to marry your teacher. And you get to be our guests!"

Twenty-two young mouths dropped open, and before they shut, all the invited adults streamed in, led by Elana's principal. One guest carried a cake, another brought nonalcoholic beverages, and Bob's mother was already aiming her handheld video camera.

Once the room settled down, Elana organized the children into a circle with the adults standing behind them. "Remember how every marriage has to have witnesses?" she asked her students. "Well, we want you to be witnesses to our marriage. Okay?"

"Yeaaah!" they shouted, filling the room with enthusiastic approval.

Elana's mother handed her a bouquet of red and white roses mixed with mistletoe to honor the couple's special commitment and new life. Then they stood in the middle of the circle, spontaneously proclaiming their love, their devotion, and their intention to live with purpose and spiritual integrity. Then Bob's uncle led them through the standard vows and the exchange of rings (simple gold bands), ending with "I now pronounce you husband and wife."

When the newlyweds kissed, the children cheered and jumped up and down and the adults filled the room with applause. When the children lined up to kiss the bride and hug the groom, even some of the men were overtaken by tear-filled joy. It was truly a magical wedding.

Another example comes from Debra Womack, who wrote,

Jamie and I were married in a national park close to home. My sweetie and I walked down the 'aisle' together. We had a cookout right there. Everyone had a great time, and we spent less than six hundred dollars. My husband and I decided that we are going to continue to have fun — being silly and just generally being in love — as long as we can, hopefully well into our nineties.

Debra and her husband focused on the joy of the celebration, the closeness of their community of loved ones, the fun of being outdoors together, and the deep satisfaction of expressing their marriage moment in a way that meant the most to them.

These are minimum-budget examples. But it doesn't matter how much you plan to spend as long as you make the meaning of the moment your highest guiding principle.

A Budget Will Keep You Honest…and Sane

Wedding fever is very common, very dangerous, and very contagious. It undermines a normally sane and stable person's capacity to evaluate the factors that are truly important to the wedding. To immunize yourself against infection, you need to determine a budget — and stick to it — no matter who will pay for your wedding. Otherwise, it's too easy to get carried away with every little detail and to be persuaded by any vendor who seems to have the very latest thing and tries to make you feel that your wedding would be nothing without it.

But before you settle on your budget, you need to determine your priorities. Here's a list of questions, focusing on the financial side of your wedding, that can help. Take turns answering them. You'll find that they echo and extend the conversation you began when discussing The Ten Key Issues of Married Life in chapter 2. If you run into conflicts, you can use this as an opportunity to hash out the values that are dearly important to each of you. Speak and listen with respect for yourselves and each other, as well as with care for your relationship.

❖ *What does "the perfect wedding" mean to you? Why?*

❖ *Are you comfortable with debt? If so, how much?*

❖ *If someone else pays for your wedding, will you feel obligated to repay them, if not financially, then emotionally? If yes, in what ways?*

❖ *Do you need your wedding to be a large production?*

❖ *Would you be comfortable with a wedding smaller than your friends' weddings?*

❖ *Would you be happy with only forty to sixty guests?*

❖ *Do you want your guests to attend both the ceremony and the reception, or just the reception?*

❖ *Do you want an expensive gown? If so, why? If no, why not?*

❖ *Is every person on your guest list someone you know and want to be there? If not, to whom are you obligated, and why? Is that obligation acceptable to you?*

❖ *How much do you expect to spend on your honeymoon? Why? Are there any alternatives to your plan?*

❖ *To begin your marriage with a stable financial foundation, are you willing to bank what you would have spent on a large wedding?*

❖ *What else belongs on your list of wedding priorities?*

We understand the almost uncontrollable impulse to pull out all the stops, never mind how much they cost, and design an event that could be in the running for the wedding industry's "gala event" Academy Award or win an Olympic medal for the most effort expended on a wedding. But that's not what smart couples do. Now that you have discussed your reasons for holding a public wedding at all — in other words, your reasons for not simply eloping — you need to address the scale of your aspirations.

As Marie told us, "If couples had their values properly in sight, they would use the $22,500 toward their future, not blow it on some dream day or on impressing the crowd." Wedding fever springs from the idea that *lavish, ostentatious*, and *outrageous* are synonymous with *perfect wedding*. But, to be fair, extravagance isn't a tendency only of modern times. Historically, the bride's father gave an all-day party with enormous amounts of food and drink, not only for the bridal party, their families, and invited guests, but also for everyone in the entire town. The feast was the way the bride's father publicly congratulated himself on the successful arrangement he had made for his daughter. He could spend lavishly because he was no longer legally or financially responsible for her.

For him, the celebration was an end in itself. For you, your wedding is just the beginning. So how can you enjoy a wonderfully romantic ceremony and celebration while starting your marriage on a solid financial footing? When you establish an absolute limit on what you are willing to spend on your wedding and your honeymoon, and you keep each other within that limit all along the way, you'll join as a team loyal to your short-term as well as long-range vision and goals. Doing so will create an emotional, intellectual, and spiritual connection — which is, after all, the heart of romance and intimacy.

Laurel and Dean's solution to the issue was to buy their home before they got married. Laughing, Laurel told us, "Go into escrow two days before your wedding — that'll keep away wedding fever for sure."

Open a Wedding Account

We assume that you, as a smart couple, take your financial future seriously. So we recommend that you open a special checking account to be used only for your wedding. Whether you're using your own money or you've decided to accept financial support from one or both sets of parents, put only your budgeted amount into this account. Then you'll know that these funds are all you have for the wedding, the reception, and the honeymoon.

Be firm with yourselves. Pay your wedding bills only out of this account. If you designate a separate credit card for wedding expenses, those charges must be paid out of this account as well. This way, it will be easier for you to keep track of everything and to stay within your budget.

Remember, money left over after you've come in under budget can go into a post-honeymoon savings account or a joint checking account.

Limit the Extras

Janie, marrying for the second time, said she'd learned her lesson: "This time with Tony, I'm bypassing all the little stuff, like the favors — everybody just leaves them behind anyway — and saving the money."

Looking back at our own wedding, we can see that our guest book was a waste of money, time, and effort. We've never even looked through it, whereas we've watched our wedding video many times. Other people told us that they shouldn't have bothered with gifts between the bride and groom, special toasting glasses, decorated sugar cubes, aisle runners, excessive food, live birds, and even balloons that were released for only a momentary dramatic effect.

As you consider the extras, ask yourselves about the reality of the romance you share. If all the small, inconsequential, and often expensive details distract you, you will miss the real thing. After all, how can you experience your romance when you allow yourselves to be guided by misplaced ambitions, peer pressure, or even your mothers' dreams — to say nothing of the fantasies ceaselessly promoted by movies, romance novels, and wedding vendors whose primary interest is *their* bottom line rather than yours? When you are smart about your money, you'll find that you can avoid the hassle and anxiety caused by fretting over every little detail.

Donna complained that on her wedding day she burst into tears while having her hair done because she still had so much to do. "Afterward it all seemed senseless because all I cared about was being with my husband and the people who were there to love and support us."

Yet surely friends have told you that their weddings were sensational because they paid so much attention to all the little details, whether they were the mauve ribbons on the programs or the sugar cubes decorated with rosebuds to match the bride's bouquet. But what do you really want everyone talking about? The food, your flowers, and the music? Or your spiritually meaningful ceremony, and the light of deep love between you and your new spouse?

Provided you chose the latter, consider these additional questions:

❖ *What details could you classify, right now, as unimportant?*

❖ *How might you reduce your florist's bill without losing the look and feel you want?*

❖ *Since food and alcohol are often the most expensive items at the reception, how might you creatively think up menu and beverage selections that will fulfill your dreams without breaking the bank?*

It's easy to follow convention and do what everyone else is doing. But when you're open to new possibilities, when you allow your imaginations to come together and inspire you, you'll discover the best ideas. And, very often, those unconventional ideas will also cost less.

Fun Alternatives

We're not at all opposed to the traditional church wedding with the reception afterward. We like the idea well enough to have done it ourselves. But wherever you choose to hold your event, we urge you to let your loving creativity lead.

To help inspire you, here are a few unique stories that people shared with us, each of which embodies rich romance and a predetermined and stuck-to budget. The first is from a magazine writer:

Because we decided to use our wedding money (ten thousand dollars from my parents and five thousand dollars from my fiancé's grandfather) as the down payment on a real estate investment — actually, a darling triplex where we got a great owner-occupied loan, and our tenants in the other units pay for our mortgage — we decided to radically simplify everything. Avoiding all the hassle and stress, we had our close family and friends meet us in Las Vegas.

The hotel where they married supplied everything, even the flowers, the cake, and the photographer. They didn't have to do anything but show up. She told us that the best part was that they could focus on themselves, the sacred moment of marrying each other, and spending lots of time with their closest loved ones.

Former clients of ours solved the budget issue by making their wedding an all-day affair:

We chose to marry at noon on the lawn at my best friend's house. Then we served brunch. The menu, executed by a small local caterer, included crepes, eggs Benedict, Belgian waffles, and lots of breakfast meats. Of course, there was tea and coffee, juices, and fresh fruit, and we served champagne. My aunt made the gorgeous four-tiered cake with rosebuds around each layer. When the party broke up at five, we left for the airport. It was all very elegant and very inexpensive compared to dinner at a hotel. Oh, and we only invited sixty people. That's the beloved inner sanctum!

When Judith was first in private practice, one of the therapists in her office suite and his fiancée planned their wedding reception around a country-western theme. They invited approximately fifty guests and held the reception in an open field in the Santa Monica mountains in Los Angeles County. The party took place after the couple and their immediate families had completed the wedding ceremony at a local Jewish temple. They asked the guests to bring dishes of Mexican food to share. The couple supplied decorations, tableware, sangria and other liquid refreshments, and the cake. A live foot-stompin' band — friends of the couple — supplied the music, and the party was a rousing success.

Whether you think this sounds cheap — or not — no one minded. It created a memorable event, and, in fact, many of us commented that we felt more involved and better able to provide real, practical help in supporting our friends as they started their new life than we would've felt at a traditional wedding.

Finally, we found this story on the Web, submitted to usabride.com by Kim:

> We had a pretty large wedding planned at first. But things got too hectic as the guest list grew and *grew*. We decided to "elope" and planned a small wedding at Lake Tahoe. We invited forty of our closest friends and family members and had the most incredible weekend.
>
> Because it was smaller, we were able to do a lot of the elegant, costly things we would not have been able to do at a bigger wedding. It also allowed us to relax and enjoy the party instead of spending all our time rotating [around] the tables. We booked a glass chapel that overlooked the lake. I asked when sunset would be on our wedding date, and planned the wedding at 8 P.M. Everyone asked us, "Why so late?"...until they saw the sunset reflecting off the lake at the same time we said, "I do." It was the most incredibly romantic thing I could have ever imagined.

Money, Money, Money

The issue of wedding costs and future finances raises the thorny question of whether you are permitted to suggest in your invitation that you'd prefer money instead of traditional wedding gifts. While the debate rages on, conventional etiquette still wins the day. So, unless and until Miss Manners and her Sisters d'Etiquette change their minds, don't mention money or gifts in the invitation. Instead, if you want to save for a house or even a trip around the world and you have all the towels and dishes you could ever want, make sure to let your family and close friends know that. When people ask them what you'd like, you'll want them to say, "They've started a savings account dedicated to the down payment for a house [or whatever], and any help you can give them would be very much appreciated."

But we take a tougher stand on the issue of money dances and money trees at receptions. Your guests have already given to you several times over. They've spent time, care, and money in selecting a wedding card and gift. No matter how cheap you might think someone's gift is, they gave what they could afford or felt was appropriate, based on how well they know you. They've also spent time, care, and money traveling to be present at your ceremony and reception. To now announce that they can pay a dollar or more to dance with either one of you, or that they should pin bills on a tree, is a bit close to prostituting yourselves on the day that is dedicated to your love.

But money-gift customs vary according to culture. In some cultures, it's a long-standing tradition for the wedding couple to give the maid of honor a specially decorated bag to carry throughout the reception, into which guests may place money gifts. Or the couple might provide something such as a decorated mailbox into which guests can spontaneously drop bills of any denomination or cards with money enclosed. But the DJ doesn't make an announcement or appeal for these monies. The money gifts are given just because everyone has done this for generations. For example, at traditional Italian weddings, guests gave money-laden envelopes to the bride as they went through the receiving line. And she thanked them with small beribboned gifts of Jordan almonds. (Some say that's how Jordan almonds became synonymous with wedding favors.)

If this type of financial giving fits your culture — certainly, in Jim's Polish family, people routinely bring money cards to everything from weddings to funerals — you will want to have a plan in place for receiving these additional gifts.

Your Personal Wealth

When you vote for your financial stability rather than a big blowout meant to impress others or to fulfill a lifelong fantasy, you support your intention to keep your love on solid ground rather than dangling precariously at the edge of emotional and financial debt. Since you are reading this book, we trust that you are, indeed, a smart couple and will make choices based on your true personal wealth — your love for each other and your desire for a successful marriage.

CHAPTER 5

Your Invitation

Since I'm an astrologer and Jason is a professional glassblower, we created our invitation with a crystal ball on the cover and the question "Where will I be on December first? (Turn the page and find out!)." Everyone loved it!

— Cheryl Johnston, astrologer, Oregon

S aturday morning, just as you finish your first cup of coffee, you decide to go for the mail. Still in your robe and slippers, second cup of coffee in hand, you stroll to the mailbox to find an oversized, overstuffed envelope ornately addressed in elegant calligraphy on creamy vellum bond. You know immediately what it is. It's an invitation. And not just any invitation. It's an invitation to a wedding.

Your invitation provides the first impression your guests receive of how your wedding will look and feel. And your invitation not only represents the two of you; it also conveys the character of your relationship, the meaning of your marriage, and the spirit of your future together.

Creatively Inviting

Beth, a personal coach, and Mark, a real estate agent, spent nearly a year planning their wedding. According to Beth, "It was a glorious time of getting to know each other better, sharing ideas about what we wanted, and pinning down exactly what would best represent us as a couple." They fully appreciated each other, turning their planning process and the decision making that it required into a romantic exploration.

In answer to the question "What should our invitation look like?" they asked Mark's sister Susanna, an artist, to create something special for them. Offering it as her wedding gift, Susanna produced a painting of two strong, jewel-colored birds seated next to each other on a branch, poised and secure, depicting a sense of vibrant and solid togetherness. That image became part of their invitation and the program for the ceremony, as well as a metaphor for their vision of their future.

The vivid birds materialized in mailboxes across the country, with a simple message printed on clear parchment attached by a blue satin ribbon to five-by-seven creamy white card stock, which read:

> *It is with great joy that*
> *Beth Davis*
> *and*
> *Mark Richter*
> *invite you to join in their wedding celebration*
> *at their home on*

Saturday, April 12, 2003, at 2 P.M.
Reception immediately following.

Their love for each other, and for everyone they included, shaped their message. Rather than predictable words — "We request the honour of your presence..." — they chose words that made their message clear. Their guests were being invited to *join* in a celebration of *great joy*. Their invitation was a personal statement expressing the way Beth and Mark felt about each other and about their wedding. Language and art combined to convey Beth and Mark's warmth and personal freedom and the festive attitude that would fill their day.

An Invitation Fit for You and Your Relationship

As Beth and Mark did, you can make your invitation a beautiful expression of yourselves and a declaration of the life and spirit of your relationship. To do that, choose to invest it with your imagination.

Of course, if you simply selected an invitation from a catalog of predesigned possibilities, your task might be considerably easier. You'd simply follow convention, and that decision would be taken care of. But what impression would your guests have when they read it? They might think that the form and style of your wedding would be the same as those of thousands before it, and that your wedding essentially would belong to someone else. It's *your* invitation. How do you want it to look, and what do you want it to say?

Before you answer that — and setting aside, for the moment, the necessary details of who, where, and when — consider the following to help you choose your wording:

❖ *What emotional tone do you want to convey about your wedding? Will it be formal and quite serious? Might it be whimsical and romantic? Or perhaps you've chosen a theme such as country-western or winter wonderland?*

❖ *How do you want your guests to dress? In long gowns and tuxedos? Cocktail dresses and dark suits? Afternoon attire? Casual clothing? In keeping with your specific theme or color combination?*

❖ *What other specific information will your guests need to help them feel comfortable at your event?*

Answering the following questions will also help you decide how you want your invitation to look:

❖ *What are your favorite colors? Perhaps this will help you decide on the paper or card stock you will use.*

❖ *What are the most important interests you and your partner share? Would you like to depict one or more of them via a photograph, sketch, or graphic design?*

❖ *Is there a symbol of your love that you both enjoy, such as roses, teddy bears, sailboats, hearts, or a special song? It might be fun to integrate this symbol into your design.*

❖ *Do you want to use a photograph of the two of you? If so, make sure that the spirit of the photo matches the style and mood of your wedding.*

If you are comfortable designing your invitation yourselves, that's great. Otherwise, get help from a friend or professional who can turn your ideas into a work of art. If you don't know anyone artistic or you have a limited budget for invitations, contact the art department at your local college and talk with a professor about your needs. No doubt she or he will know a student who would be glad to help for a small fee and/or to be able to add your invitation to their portfolio.

Perhaps you want to choose a very formal, traditional approach to your invitations. If so, be sure that your choice is an expression of your deepest beliefs. There is much to be said for tradition. That's why it lasts for decades, even centuries. When you make tradition part of who you are through your own understanding and interpretation, you will feel assured that it fits your dreams and values.

Designing and planning your wedding is not a time to compete with your friends. You know what we mean — trying to make your invitation bigger, better, more beautiful, or whatever. To truly enjoy your wedding process, focus on the elements that best represent the two of you and the kind of wedding and marriage that *you* are creating. Your wedding is a special and sacred event — even if it is completely secular — so take the time to make your invitation as meaningful to you both as you can.

Words of Love in Purple

With that in mind, we pulled out our memory book to look at our own invitation. It was larger than Judith remembered and lighter in color than Jim recalled. We were delighted with what we had created seventeen years ago. Seeing it was such a pleasure — we were inspired to look through both our wedding and honeymoon albums, cherishing once again how beautifully we had expressed the feeling and meaning of our wedding journey.

For our invitation, we had used five-by-seven mauve card stock and arranged a set of words, in purple ink, in the form of a large heart. The words epitomized the core values of our marriage: *Caring, Support, Passion, Wholeness, Empathy, Tenderness,*

Inspiration, Companionship, Respect, Understanding, Intimacy, Sexuality, Commitment, Fulfillment, Acceptance, Play, and *Freedom.* Above the heart we had written "Judith & Jim," and inside it "Invite You to Join in Celebration of Their Marriage"; the date, time, place; and "Reception Immediately Following the Ceremony." Below the heart we'd added "Light Hors d'Oeuvres Buffet" and "Be Sure to Bring Your Dancing Shoes." The style and tone were meant to convey our desire for a relaxed and intimate wedding ceremony and a fun party afterward.

Be sure your invitation makes you feel good about yourselves and makes the people who will receive them feel good about being included. As a final test, imagine it's your twenty-fifth wedding anniversary and you open your wedding album to reminisce. Will your invitation still make you smile and want to hold hands?

Embrace Your Guests

Just as you need to be respectful of yourselves, you need to be respectful of your guests. After all, your invitation will be addressed to them. Will they easily understand your message? Are not only the words but the intentions of your message spelled out clearly?

When we planned our reception, we had two goals in mind. We didn't want to follow a preplanned schedule. Instead we wanted a lively party. And we didn't want people to find themselves stuck at formal tables that made it difficult for them to move around, mingle, and dance.

So, in describing the food that our caterer would serve, we purposely chose the words "Light Hors d'Oeuvres Buffet," thinking this would make it clear to everyone that we wouldn't have a formal sit-down dinner. Our caterer agreed. But we didn't call any of our friends and ask them how they interpreted that description. Big mistake.

Here's what happened. Many of our guests ate dinner before they arrived. Why? Because they knew that we loved to dance and that we loved funky blues and rock music. So they assumed that we would have a rock-out band, which we did. Expecting to dance the night away, they interpreted our wording to mean that we'd provide little more than snacks to sustain them during the later hours. But what the caterer had prepared, albeit still in the finger-food category, was more than enough to be a casual ongoing dinner — which is what we had intended — to say nothing of the beer, wine, and champagne we offered. Many guests were disappointed that they weren't hungry. And we were shocked by the amount of food we paid for that went uneaten.

So be sure that your invitation will speak clearly to your guests. In fact, you might want to ask an informal focus group of friends whether they understand your wording. Your guests need to understand the facts of your event, how to dress, and what they can expect. And they want to feel embraced by the manner in which you invite them.

Who Are the Hosts?

If you follow conventional wedding etiquette, your parents, whether just the bride's or the bride's and the groom's, will host your wedding day. And if that's the case, their names will come first on your invitation:

> *Mr. and Mrs. John Doe*
> *request the honor of your presence*
> *at the marriage of their daughter...*

This tradition originated at a time when most couples married young and a man had to seek permission from his sweetheart's father before he proposed. And since women were not allowed to initiate proposals, they certainly weren't allowed to host their own weddings. Consequently, until the twentieth century, most American weddings took place at the bride's parents' home. So it made sense that her parents would be the hosts and that they would send out the invitations.

If that still makes sense and feels right for the two of you, then by all means have one or both sets of parents host your wedding, and word your invitation accordingly. But we hope that you are ready to publicly proclaim your own readiness for married life by inviting your guests yourselves. After all, it's your future that you are stepping into. Why shouldn't the two of you make the first public announcement of that step?

That's what Steve and Patty did. He lived in California and she lived in South Dakota, and they met online. Their relationship was guided by humorous repartee right from the beginning. After several plane flights in each direction, punctuated by teary airport good-byes, they knew something had to change.

Here's how they expressed their love and desire to be together:

Given our overwhelming inability
to exist 1,307 miles apart and
in the interest of good taste
and public decency, we,
Steven Kent Marshall
and
Patricia Ann Miller,
have decided that we must marry.
We'd love for you to attend.

Monday, December 21, 1998 — 4 P.M.
at the
Spearfish Canyon Lodge
Spearfish Canyon, South Dakota
(Grub following the ceremony.)
No gifts, please!
We have enough stuff already.

Then There's Your Guest List

Franca, twenty-four, and Benji, thirty, held their ceremony and reception in a grand old barn in upstate New York. "The very best thing about our wedding was that everyone there was someone who knew us and loved us very much. We were lifted up from beginning to end by the group's joy and excitement for us."

It's your wedding. Follow Franca and Benji's model by inviting those who support you, who wish you well, and who love you. Invite the people you love and enjoy. Put those people on your A list. You can place other potential guests on a B list. When reviewing the B list and considering whom to invite, ask yourselves:

❖ *Will this person add to our pleasure and the meaning of our wedding?*

❖ *Would we miss this person if she or he wasn't able to attend?*

❖ *Do we feel pressure from friends or family to invite this person?*

❖ *Are we concerned about hurting this person's feelings by not inviting her or him?*

❖ *Will this person rejoice in celebrating with us?*

❖ *Will she or he be likely to disturb other people by being rowdy or offensive?*

If you know that some guests are likely to get drunk or act up or you're anxious about what they might do, think very seriously about whether to include them, whether they're family or friends. If you're worried about hurting someone's feelings, remember that your wedding is not a charity event — it's not your job to protect everyone from the truth of your choices.

It's true that your reception will be a party of sorts, but that is only its superficial aspect. At its heart, it will be a celebration of the joining of your lives — a celebration that will be based in love, support, and positive intentions for your future. Treat it with spiritual respect, and honor yourselves by choosing to invite only those who will do the same.

In some instances, when parents have divorced, bringing them together for the wedding can be uncomfortable, if not painful. If you're in this situation, we know how hard it must be. If you are certain that their presence will not be a distraction, then by all means invite them both. But if you're uncertain, opt for what you need. You were not responsible for their divorce, so don't assume responsibility for inviting them just because you're "supposed to." If you've remained close to both parents, then take responsibility for yourself by speaking with them and making sure that they promise to be on their best behavior. Their job is to support you, not the other way around.

The best wedding gift you can give yourselves is to take on the role of *adults* rather than to be good *children*. If friends or family members pressure you to invite people you'd rather not, we strongly urge you to hold your ground unless there's very good reason to comply. Not only will this protect your wedding from intrusion, you'll also get to practice standing up for yourselves, which will be necessary in your marriage. After all, you'll need to stand up for yourselves in order to successfully blend your differences without either of you becoming lost in the mix.

As you make your final guest-list decisions, it will help to remember that your choices will indicate the lifestyle you are choosing for your future. Your choice of guests will suggest the kind of future social circle you envision as well as your role in it. So choose those who respect and cherish you. You will then be using even your guest list as a way to say that your first loyalty is to your relationship and your marriage.

RSVPs

If you plan to serve anything beyond cake and punch at your reception, you'll need to know how many people will attend. Yet getting accurate and prompt responses from guests is a widespread problem, so much so that the Dear Abby and Ann Landers columns repeatedly address difficulties with RSVPs.

You can protect yourselves, to a large degree, through a mature and self-respectful approach. First, invite people you know want to come. Our survey respondents, male and female alike, were quite clear in expressing their displeasure at wedding invitations that were used, at least in part, as a tool of family politics. They wanted to know that they had been invited because the bride or groom (or both) truly valued them and wanted the pleasure of their attendance. No doubt, many who fail to RSVP are stating their displeasure at being invited for the wrong reasons.

Second, don't hesitate to call or email anyone who doesn't respond by your due date. You are not being rude when you contact them to request an answer. They are being rude by not responding.

Your invitation is more than merely an announcement and a request that people attend your wedding. It symbolizes who the two of you are together. It graphically portrays the essence of your relationship and represents the spirit of your love and desire for the future.

So, any way the two of you choose to create your invitation, let it stand as a mark of personal expression and a loving welcome to all those you want to be with you on your special day.

CHAPTER 6

Parties Are a Preview

It touched me so much that my very best friends created not just a shower, with gifts and a great lunch, but they made it into a really special time of saying farewell to being single.

— Jillian Baxter, cardiologist, New York

*P*rewedding parties often preview your postwedding social life: they suggest who you will have as friends, where you will go, and how you will celebrate life's passages. They offer an excellent opportunity to make sure that the two of you are celebrated in a manner that fits your spiritual values, psychological needs, and future goals and dreams. Thus, they can also preview another aspect of your future — the ease or difficulty you might have in stating and claiming what you want and need. So, when someone wants to host a party for you, describe what kind of party would be especially meaningful to you. Give the host clear guidelines for what you want or don't want, who you want invited or not.

Several years ago, Kathryn, a twenty-eight-year-old professional, told us that she was off to Chicago for a bridal shower that her Lithuanian aunts were giving her. She didn't seem too happy about it and told us she didn't really want to go. Her grandmother, who was from the old country, also demanded that she bring along Roger, her fiancé.

"They're not bad people," she sighed. "It's just their tradition. In my family the aunts are supposed to give the shower. But they never bothered to ask me if I wanted one in Chicago."

"Why not tell them how you feel?"

"Oh, I couldn't do that. They're expecting me."

"How does Roger feel about it?"

"He doesn't know yet. I'm afraid to tell him. He's English and somewhat reserved. There'll be so much kissing and hugging, it scares me to imagine what he might think."

The issue wasn't whether Kathryn and Roger would go to Chicago. It was Kathryn's reticence to say what she felt, especially to Roger.

"Do you know what you are saying to yourself?" we asked her. "That you'd rather hide from your own truth and from Roger. That's no way to start a marriage. Besides, there'll be many more instances when you will need to speak your mind. If you don't, you'll undermine yourself and your marriage, and your children if you have any. Is that what you want?"

Speaking up for things that are meaningful to you is part of the foundation of a successful marriage. You can practice by making certain that the parties given in your honor are as you want them to be.

Kathryn and Roger did go to Chicago, and they had a wonderful time. But they went only after she had had a long talk with her mother, who had just assumed that Kathryn would want the same kind of shower that had been given for all the other brides in the family. Since Kathryn had been the only one of her generation to move away, she had to help her mother understand who she'd become. In the end, her mother thanked her for respecting her aunts and grandmother, and told her she was proud of what Kathryn had accomplished. The Chicago shower was a gift in more ways than one.

So, what could make *your* parties particularly special?

Bridal Showers

Traditionally, bridal showers meant casual conversation, party games, cake and punch, and, of course, gifts, because historically gifts were what showers were all about. But how might you expand on this tradition?

Most brides want to be celebrated with fancy, beautifully gift-wrapped surprises, which might even be essential to starting a first home. But what, specifically, might you want to include that would deepen the powerful importance of the parties given for you, parties meant to honor your rite of passage from single-hood to married life?

A Shower of Memories

At the shower will be guests you've known for years and years, and a few you might have just met. There will be guests from your family, work, church, school, and perhaps even the neighborhood where you grew up. Gathered together will be a rich collection of perspectives on who you are and what you have meant to each guest. So wouldn't it be fun if your host(s) included in the invitation a request that each guest bring a favorite memory of you, a short story that epitomizes who you are for her? Then, before you unwrap each person's material gift, that person could share her special story about you as an additional touching or humorous gift of love.

Not only will this save the guests from forced and extended conversation with strangers, it will unite them in their celebration of you. You will not only be supplied with toasters and negligees, you will be gifted with memorable stories of love from those who hold you dear.

The Prayerful Shower

Perhaps best suited for the shower given by your church friends and/or family members who all share the same religious faith, prayerful blessings from each guest can be requested in the invitation by the host(s). Depending on your religious practice and the size of the guest list, guests could offer their prayers for your future marriage before the refreshments are served. Or blessings could accompany the unwrapping of gifts.

Prayers need not be stodgy or even taken from religious texts. Some people might find simple lines from a song, a novel, or a play that speak volumes. Others might want to read you a few short lines from their favorite book of poetry. And many prayers are best said in one's own words, straight from the heart.

A shower supported by prayerful blessings contributes religious meaning to the mundane — it adds angel wings to the kitchen towels. And it reminds all who participate that a marriage rich in love is a romantic tapestry in which everyday events and divine meaning are woven together.

The Mystical Shower

This shower is perfect for you if you value the metaphysical. The host(s) of your Mystical Shower invites each guest to bring a fortune-telling tool to the party. Whether it's numerology, a brief astrological reading, the I Ching or Runes, or tarot, angel, or oracle cards, each guest will give you a short reading.

Kayla, twenty-six, an elementary school teacher in upstate New York, was concerned that some of her friends might not feel comfortable preparing a reading on their own. So her sister, the maid of honor, made certain to bring several books of wisdom readings to the party. Sure enough, three of the guests opted to flip to a random page, arbitrarily point to a passage, and then read it aloud. Kayla told us that each of the readings in some way addressed a nagging question about the challenge of becoming the stepmother to her soon-to-be-husband's two children.

To top it off, Kayla's aunt Fran, who collects crystals, had Kayla pull a crystal from her collection, which Fran keeps in a blue velvet bag. Because Kayla pulled out a pink agate, Fran told her to expect her experience with the children to be very positive. It would improve her vitality and energy and increase her self-confidence. Fran also said that Kayla could expect enjoyment in her new role and a new sense of balance in her life.

Rooted in ancient spirituality, this type of party celebrates the magic and unfolding adventure that marriage is sure to bring.

The Readiness Shower

Usually, anyone invited to a bridal shower has known the guest of honor long enough to have received her generosity, compassion, and maybe even help. Certainly, generosity, compassion, and helpfulness are keystones to a successful marriage, as both husband and wife need to be kind and caring helpmates to each other. The Readiness Shower honors your necessary and well-practiced ability to be helpful and kind to others — in this case, the guests.

Within the invitation, the host(s) requests that each guest

bring a brief story of a time when you were particularly helpful, thoughtful, or generous. If they are typed or written out, these stories can be glued into a special book as a keepsake. Hearing others give witness to some of your best qualities will help you center yourself, giving you well-founded confidence and assurance that you are, indeed, ready to take those forthcoming vows.

This type of shower is appropriate for both the bride and the groom. One couple — Marcie, thirty, and Gordon, twenty-eight — who came to us for premarital counseling found the Readiness Shower very helpful. Their main problem was Gordon's mother, who was worried, claiming that he "wasn't mature enough for the responsibilities of marriage." It sounded to us more like Gordon's mother was unhappy to lose her son to his own independent life, so we suggested that they ask their maid of honor and best man to give them a Readiness Shower. Afterward, Marcie and Gordon couldn't thank us enough. Their Readiness Shower provided a forum for their friends and other members of their families to give a bold and clear go-ahead, as a solidly supportive community, to their upcoming wedding.

Showers for the Bride and Groom

Showers for the couple are becoming increasingly popular. They highlight the true nature of the wedding journey: the joining of two separate lives into one combined household and life together.

Typically, guests are asked to bring gender-neutral gifts such as gardening tools or travel paraphernalia to these events. Aside from the gifts, these celebrations have been little different from any other type of party given on behalf of the bride and groom. But since couples are more sophisticated these days, and since both partners usually have quite clearly defined identities and lifestyles that need to be integrated into the oneness of marriage, joint showers are a perfect opportunity to celebrate the couple's future and to help them make a successful start before they say, "I do."

The Gotta Leave Home Shower

The Bible says it best: "Leave thy father and thy mother and cleave one unto another." It doesn't say, "Drive yourselves crazy and fight over whose parents you have to be loyal to." Nor does it say, "Become one mushy, entangled mess of lost identities in order to keep the peace." It says you have to leave home and honor your marriage as your primary family.

But you don't have to stop speaking to your parents. The point is to have the best of both worlds — a fabulous marriage *and* great relationships with all your relatives. What's the best way to get off to the right start? The laughter and tears of a Gotta Leave Home Shower.

A leaving-home shower includes all close family members: the bride's and groom's parents, stepparents, grandparents, siblings, and anyone else who is as close as a relative. While material gifts might or might not be part of this party, its centerpiece is the special time set aside for family members to honor the couple by verbally or symbolically surrendering their emotional claim on the bride or groom. In other words, each person, in their own way, acknowledges that the new marriage will come before their own tie to the bride or groom.

As you receive these tender and unselfish gifts, you both will want to demonstrate your gratitude to each speaker. Make sure you cherish their capacity to surrender you to your new life, their respect for your decision to start a new family, and their deep love, expressed through their generous gifts of heart and soul.

The Gotta Leave Home Shower offers an "extended" blessing: your entire family group joins together to cut the old ties that could unconsciously bind the two of you to the past leaving you confused and frustrated. At the same time, the entire group embraces the love-filled spiritual adventure of opening themselves to the future and forming new relationships with one another, based on respect and value for your new marriage.

The Master Mind Shower

The author Napoleon Hill and many others have reminded us that "when two or more are gathered together" for a specific and shared purpose, magical things can occur. The term "Master Mind Group" was coined by Hill: these groups, countless numbers of which have been formed all over the world, bring people together to create success for one member or for the whole group.

The host(s) of a Master Mind Shower issues invitations indicating that the event's purpose is to support the two of you in your short- and long-term goals. Guests provide help by offering gifts of talent, skill, and anything else that can help you achieve material, emotional, and spiritual success.

The invitation will include your shared goals as a couple. So this party provides a perfect opportunity for the two of you to discuss those goals beforehand, and to clearly spell out where you will be headed after you're back from your honeymoon and your thank-you notes are in the mail. If you haven't given much thought to your dreams and desires for the future, begin right now to outline your path, to make sure your marriage won't flounder from lack of direction.

As you talk about your goals, remember that your serious ambitions, whether they're monetary, professional, creative, and/or parental, can coexist with more playful ideas such as travel and hobbies. And don't forget to talk about your spiritual pursuits and your sense of a greater life purpose.

At the party itself, your entire list of goals will be displayed on poster boards or flip charts or in whatever manner the host(s) and/or the two of you choose. Preferably before refreshments, the new Master Mind Group (or whatever you wish to call it) will be called to order for its first "board of directors" meeting. No doubt you know someone who is great at energizing a group and running a meeting. Choose that person to be your chairperson.

The chair will read each goal aloud, and then the two of you will describe your intentions in detail and state what you need in order to make them a success. The point is to include your friends and family in your intentions so that they can help in as many ways as possible.

Then, after all your goals have been spelled out, the chair will guide everyone in masterminding their gift-giving. The chair will help the group think through how they might serve the two of you in reaching your goals.

Skills in accounting, real estate, banking, or brokering mortgages would be perfect to help you with a start-up business or in buying your first home. Personal coaching sessions, depending on the coach's background and orientation, could help you with career change, pursuing promotions, health issues, weight loss, fitness, or rooting out resistance to change. Offers could range from catering the grand opening of a business to babysitting while one or both of you attend college or graduate-school courses, do classwork, or take training classes. Some people might feel that their best offering to you would be their spiritual energies, prayers, and positive imaging of the two of you accomplishing your goals.

Nothing is too mundane or too wild a gift at this kind of party. The sky's the limit, since the point is to join the heavenly forces of love to your earthly goals as a soon-to-be-married couple. And there is no greater gift than your community's powerful combined support of your dreams.

Bachelor Parties

The number one complaint from our survey respondents was the stag party:

> *"The whole bachelor-party thing is totally unsupportive. Who needs that type of temptation?"*
>
> *"It's a way for the groom to cheat on his bride before they even get started."*
>
> *"Why celebrate the perceived loss of 'freedom' instead of the new life ahead?"*
>
> *"It's horrible to feel you have to have a 'last single hoorah' before the 'ball-and-chain.'"*

So what's a fellow to do?

Remember, create your wedding experience in your way. It doesn't matter what the best man might have in mind for you. Nor is what your cousin did last year for his bachelor party relevant. All that matters is that you feel comfortable and sure that your celebration with your buddies will not be contrary to your self-respect or the marriage vows you are about to make.

Since you are aware that your wedding process is, in part, a rehearsal for your marriage, be sure that you take charge of this evening. Don't be dragged into anything you'd rather not do. And, during the party itself, make sure you take the time to publicly thank the men who are there for you, who care enough to be part of your special event. Also, bachelor parties should be scheduled at least three days — if not a couple of weeks — before the rehearsal dinner so that everyone will be well rested and energized for the wedding.

With that in mind, here are some ideas that might fit your bachelor-party bill.

The Roast

Most men enjoy taking a ribbing. It's a grand old male sport. Men know it's their buddies' way of saying, "I love you, I respect you enough to poke fun at you, and I know you're man enough to take it the right way." Therefore, dinner in a restaurant's or club's private room, accompanied by roasting the groom — particularly about any eccentricities that his marriage will challenge — might be the perfect adios to single life and a friendly induction into matrimony.

If a roast appeals to you, let your best man know. When he extends the invitations, it's important that he stress that the roasting should be supportive, never hostile. He should also keep the alcohol flow moderate and schedule the roast fairly early in the evening so that everyone will be reasonably sober. Your best man should chair the roast. Prepare yourself to fully participate in the give-and-take between you and each of your courageous and friendly roasters.

Wine Tasting

If you think of yourself as sophisticated, a classy wine tasting in a fine restaurant during a seven- or even nine-course meal might be an elegant way to shift from footloose and eligible to taken-for-life-by-the-love-of-your-life.

Your best man might wish to suggest that the men arrive prepared with a toast that is especially appropriate for you. Take a look at some of the suggestions under "Bridal Showers," earlier in this chapter — depending on your personality, some of the suggestions offered there, such as guests relating stories and memories about your capacity for generosity and helpfulness, might provide a fitting theme.

Hangin' Out

Certainly, there's nothing wrong with just hanging out with your best friends. Whether you enjoy playing poker, bowling, watching a sports event on TV, or anything else, it's not *what* you do on your bachelor night that's important. It's the spirit and intention of the event. And as long as your and your friends' intention is to celebrate you and your coming wedding, that's all that matters.

The Golf Weekend

Perhaps an evening event isn't enough to signal the end of your bachelorhood. Maybe you'd like to do something athletic. What could be better than getting away for a golf weekend with your best friends?

Of course, golf might not be your thing — maybe it's surfing, tennis, hiking, or fishing. Or, in the winter, a ski weekend could symbolize the end of all those long, lonely, and cold nights alone.

When you gather together, your best man should remind everyone that the goal for the weekend is to send you into matrimony with positive support, even though you'll also focus on the sport you've chosen. Toasts and/or memorable stories about you are in order.

Parties Celebrate Who You Are Becoming

Parties are a preview of your life to come. They give friends and family an opportunity to show their special love and support as they celebrate your journey to the altar. And they give everyone an opportunity to formally recognize and honor the changes already happening in all your relationships as you shift your allegiance from yourself as a single person to the couple you will become.

These parties allow those closest to you to provide various material and spiritual gifts as you prepare to settle into the life of a married couple. But they also offer rich opportunities for you and your partner to practice feeling worthy of vast love and care, and to demonstrate that you are mature enough to fully embrace the experience of marriage.

CHAPTER 7

To Change Names, or Not?

When I decided to keep my name, so many people tried to scare me by saying I was emasculating my husband-to-be.

— Carol Hyams, corporate executive, Toronto

*I*t's still pretty much assumed that a bride will take her husband's surname. If she doesn't, people wonder why. If the groom chooses to hyphenate his name with hers, jointly take a completely new name, or take her name, he risks betraying all that has been understood as masculine.

But it's only a name. Or is it?

Her Identity

Apart from women's liberation and more than mere choice, the name the bride assumes is a statement about not only her identity but also her relationship. And as wedding traditions continue to evolve and change, the issue of married names has become more relevant for the groom as well. For the most part, however, social pressure still insists that the bride relinquish her maiden name and adopt the name of her husband. This practice dates back to a time when, although a woman had a first name, she had no *legal* name in her own right. Legally, she was known as her father's daughter, brother's sister, son's mother, or husband's wife.

As recently as the middle of the twentieth century, an article in newspaper society pages might mention that a Mrs. John Smith was the head of the committee for the beautification of the town art museum, or that a Mrs. Michael Thompson had accepted a position with a notable charity, or that Mr. and Mrs. Arthur Weber were proud to announce the engagement of their daughter. Not only the woman's maiden name but her first name was completely absent. This custom was so common and so accepted that it went unnoticed. Only in the latter part of the century did things begin to change because, for many women, this type of disappearing act was no longer very appealing.

In today's world, many women develop prestigious reputations in their own names before they marry. In Judith's case, she had a long-standing professional reputation as Judith Sherven. She didn't want to take a last name — Sniechowski — that was difficult in itself or to deal with the disruption a name change would have on her practice as a psychotherapist. Other women simply prefer an identity separate from that of "the Mrs."

Changing Her Name

Most people take marriage-related name changes for granted. They think of them as just a matter of filing the appropriate documents, and that's that. But there are many and varied reasons that people do or do not change their names.

A friend of ours, a fellow author who is also an actress and media personality, told us her story:

> When I first started modeling and acting, my agent called to tell me that my birth name, Cynthia Abruzzini, wasn't working because it was too ethnic. So I went by my first and middle names, Cynthia Lee. Then my agent said everyone thought I was Chinese.
>
> In the meantime, I married my husband, Brian. When my agent heard my married name, Cynthia Sheaff (pronounced like "beef"), he hated it. He wanted something simple and easy to pronounce. He suggested that I use my husband's first name, Brian, as my last name. Even though I chose Sheaff as my name on our marriage certificate, professionally I work under the name Cynthia Brian.
>
> It's been great for me. But my poor husband. When people assume that I took his last name, they call him Brian Brian.

Melanie Hodge kept her maiden name for her work as a massage therapist. She was delighted to tell us that "*Hodge* rhymes with 'massage.' It helps potential clients remember me." But when she began seeing Brian Garcia, her mother told her that her maternal great-grandmother had come from Spain and that her maiden name was, coincidentally, Garcia. For Melanie, family was very important, and having both her great-grandmother's and her husband's name at the same time meant a lot to her. So when she married Brian, she legally took his name.

When we asked Brian how he felt about it, he said, "It was fine with me. If she'd wanted to hyphenate it, that would've been okay. It's not something that defines us." Brian's example of open-hearted flexibility is a sign of the growing masculine security and self-confidence that increasingly allow marital name changes to be optional rather than mandatory.

Yet some people take a very strong stand. Chris Cahill, who took her husband's last name, said, "If you get married, then you should change your name.... If you are getting married, then you should be one in all ways."

While we too believe in the oneness inherent in marriage, we caution against being one in all ways. Far too often, this idea leads people to lose themselves in marriage. They give themselves over to their partners and vanish in their own right. The lifeblood of the relationship is diluted because there are no longer two separate and distinct individuals to keep the partnership exciting, compelling, and growing. Furthermore, why is it assumed that the *man's* name represents oneness? Why not hers? After all, they would still share one name.

Some women told us that they changed their names simply because they'd never liked their maiden name — it was too complicated, too weird, too something — and marriage gave them the opportunity to finally be graced by a lovely name such as Millian or Smartley or Loveland.

From Nancy Dowell, also known as Mrs. Barry C. Dowell, we received a very tender story supporting brides who take their husbands' names:

My husband was twenty-one and I had just turned twenty-three when we were married. It was still morning after we had exchanged vows at the courthouse. My new husband said he had a surprise for me. He drove me to the Motor Vehicle Administration office in Largo, Maryland, near my old high school. "Why here?" I asked him. I was wearing an all-white dress that came down over my knees, and he had on a suit! We looked overdressed for the Motor Vehicle Administration.

Then he told me the most romantic thing I could have heard. He wanted me to change my driver's license so he could see my new name on something official. We got to do something one-hour-old newlyweds rarely do!

I still think it's the sweetest thing ever. He's a man of few words, but I could tell he was really proud to share his name with me.

Still in the Process

Remember Sondra and Aaron, the couple who took their vows at the ruins of Machu Picchu? Sondra's last name is Van Ert. Aaron's is Blaker. "We thought about Blakert," Aaron said, "but my dad didn't like that." "So," Sondra said, "for now, we've decided to go with Van Ert Blaker to sort of meet midway." Aaron clarified that there was no hyphen, "just our two names together."

"But most of our friends refer to us as the Van Blakers," laughed Sondra. "Which could turn into VanAker," Aaron chimed in.

Sondra and Aaron are experiencing the grace of allowing themselves to be in process. There's no tension, no fuss; simply the pleasure of playing with their changing identities through their name(s).

The Hyphen Did It

Andy and Olivia talked very little about the name issue. It was clear that Olivia wasn't going to change her name. "Our relationship is a partnership," Andy said. "We were entering marriage together, merging our two families. We wanted to show that." Olivia told us:

> Our choice to be Olivia and Andy Cohen-Cutler was a source of great discomfort for Andy's family, and his sisters were offended by it.
>
> But for me it was an issue of identity. I am the only child of Holocaust survivors. My name is a source of pride. So I never thought about changing it. When we married, I was a feminist in law school, so my choice to hyphenate our names wasn't so unusual. But when Andy chose to do it, too, that was extraordinary.
>
> Most people we knew, including my parents, weren't surprised. My mother thought our name was cool, and while my dad was a bit puzzled, he really appreciated how we had honored his name. But Andy's mom refused to call us anything but Mr. and Mrs. Andy Cutler — for more than fifteen years. Even when our son, Donald Cohen-Cutler, arrived six years into our marriage, Andy's mother insisted on addressing packages to "Donald Cutler."

"And I still get some grief when people learn that my name is hyphenated," Andy groaned.

In speaking with the Cohen-Cutlers, it was obvious that Olivia felt blessed to be with a man who would join her so totally in such a personal issue, even brooking his mother's disregard and other people's odd reactions. "Andy did it. That was what was so impressive." It is obvious that Olivia is still very much in love with the guy on the other side of the hyphen.

Changing His Name

At a backyard barbecue given by friends of ours, Rachel Sherstack told us that she'd divorced the father of her baby Christopher. The marriage was "a short-lived mistake of youth." Since her ex had disappeared shortly after Christopher's birth, she had taken back her maiden name for both of them.

Soon after the divorce, she met the man who would be her true marriage partner, Randy Flowers. Randy had never liked his last name. "My dad beat me and called me 'Pansy Flowers.' I haven't seen him since I went away to college. And my mom died a couple of years after that. When I proposed to Rachel, I also proposed that I change my name to hers. I didn't want Christopher to have a different name or to have to suffer the confusion, at three, of getting a new name. I also wanted our children to have the same name as Christopher."

"If I'd had any doubt about Randy's willingness to take on a three-year-old son along with a new marriage, our discussion about his changing his name was the most romantic gift he could have given me," Rachel said, holding their baby girl, Ashleen, while Randy bounced Christopher on his knee.

Keeping Her Name

Erin Saxton, whom we've known since she was the producer for our first appearance on *The View*, didn't change her last name when she married Anders Bjornson because she had a formidable string of credits as a television producer. Continuing to work in the media, she has recently added credits as a casting director to her professional résumé and has independently established her own media/PR company, The Idea Network.

Michelle Hoyt, the daughter of a friend, wrote, "I am thirty-three years old, and I simply think it would be difficult to change the only name I've ever known. I discussed this with my fiancé even before he was my fiancé, and he is fine with it. I asked him (and other men), 'Would you change your name to your new wife's name just because you loved her so much?' Every man I asked said *no!* So why is it different for a woman? My name is who I am."

Deborah Genovesi relayed an even stronger sentiment about why she had kept her name:

> My husband and I dated for two years and then were engaged for three more before we married. And no, it was not the usual case of the groom-to-be harboring a deep fear of commitment. It was me, the bride, who was commitment-phobic! Eventually I came around.
>
> During our long courtship, we discussed anything and everything — we have always been great communicators — and that has helped us tremendously in our marriage. The issue of whether I would change my name was really a nonissue. We both hold strong feminist ideals and feel that losing one's name signifies a loss of independence and hints at male domination.
>
> I was already in my late twenties and established in the business world under my name [when we married]. I am proud of its ethnic ring, and it is a deeply ingrained part of who I am. I've always felt that when a married woman takes her husband's name, she is in fact being

branded as his property, rather like livestock. It's like the husband is declaring, "This is my truck, my cow, my wife." The whole concept smacks of ownership and didn't feel right to either of us.

We realize this is not a traditional point of view, and over the years I have come under scrutiny, even by my own father, whose name I kept, for choosing to do something so "radical."

My husband actually offered to take my family's name. I wouldn't let him do so, for the same reasons. He isn't my property any more than I am his. We briefly discussed creating a new, hybrid name with elements from each of our last names but decided that would be too unwieldy and confusing, as would hyphenating.

As we began to plan our wedding, we made it clear to all involved that I would not be changing my name. I repeatedly reviewed that with our minister, who forgot and announced us as "Mr. and Mrs. Laskos" at the church, much to my dismay.

It's interesting to note that even eleven years later I still get comments on our different last names. I've had several people tell me that my maiden name was not legal once I got married — which is entirely false. Occasionally people are confused as to whether we are actually married, which is understandable. Some — mostly women, interestingly — have commented that if I really loved my husband, I would have taken his name. Many have chided me that should we ever decide to have children, this arrangement will be a disaster.

Just this year, my father, whom I love dearly, asked me, "When are you going to stop this women's lib nonsense and just take Walter's name?" I've even lost friends over this issue. One particular out-of-town friend insisted on addressing her mail to "Mrs. Laskos" instead of "Ms. Genovesi." After several years of corrections and a lengthy discussion, she told me she thought I was ridiculous and continued to send mail addressed incorrectly — mail I eventually sent back, marked "Return to sender. No one at this address by that name." The friendship fizzled after I decided that someone who would so blatantly ignore my point of view wasn't worth having in my life.

I do find it both interesting and curious that this is such a volatile issue in our culture and that most criticism comes from women and is directed at the wife. Hillary Rodham came under attack for keeping her name and eventually had to bite the bullet and drop it for the good of her husband's campaign. Teresa Heinz had to add "Kerry" when his presidential bid required it.

I don't hold any ill will toward women who decide to change their names when they get married. I don't understand why anyone would want to do so, but I feel it is their prerogative. Changing one's name is a personal choice, and that is my point — we all have a *choice*. If it is meaningful to you to take your husband's name, then by all means have at it. Just don't call me "Mrs. Laskos"!

As Deborah says, whether to change names can be one of the more controversial issues when you marry on your own terms. However, if we, as a society, insist on imposing the values of our ancestors on today's couples, we support a tradition that can undermine the evolution of self-awareness and individuality that are essential to the well-being of each partner and the success of their marriage.

Making Your Decision Together

There are many reasons why you might want to change your name, and just as many why you might not. Whatever your decision, make it with serious consideration.

Traditionally, it has been the bride who has changed her name. So here we include an exercise for you, the bride. Yet it applies equally to the groom. Both of you can answer the questions below and discuss them together.

❖ *Write your name in each of the possible forms we just reviewed — taking the groom's name, creating a new name from both of yours, hyphenating your names, changing the groom's name to the bride's, and keeping the bride's name.*

❖ *Say each of these out loud.*

❖ *Delete any that are out of the question for you.*

❖ *Jointly discuss the remaining options. Talk about all of the names' ramifications — their effects on your families and friends, your work life, your children's last name(s), what each choice means to you, as well as anything else that the names could affect.*

❖ *Now, which name(s) makes you feel most at home, most comfortable, and proudest?*

There is no need to make a final decision now. The important thing is to mull your options over until both of you feel empowered by and strongly identified with the name(s) you will select.

Respecting and valuing your uniqueness, and knowing your own private and public reasons for your choice, will make the naming process more meaningful and will deepen your pride and comfort in the name you will be known by for the rest of your life.

CHAPTER 8

The Case for Prenups and Financial Planning

I am happy to say that we spent a lot of time preparing for our future together by taking classes, reading books, and spending many hours engaged in conversation about the growth and nurturance of being married — actively married, not married as a destination but as a life path, with our eyes and attention on the here and now as well as on the road ahead.

— Nick Rath, parent education teacher, California

While planning your wedding might be the highlight of your relationship so far, it is merely the beginning. There is much more to come. As unromantic as it might sound, the fact is that you're creating not only a marriage but also a business relationship that will continually process cash coming in and cash going out. And that fact is best discussed ahead of time. Why? Because in the eyes of the law, you are entering into a legally recognized financial partnership. That partnership can have serious consequences — for better and for worse.

Planning Ahead

Now is the time, while you are planning your wedding and your married life to follow, to face an aspect of marriage that far too many couples avoid: money! Through premarital financial planning, you can head off the unnecessary money problems that disrupt and even dissolve many marriages. We don't intend to introduce frustration or more hassle into your wedding plans, but we encourage you to think beyond your wedding day. Financial planning will make your (and your partner's) relationship to money, your goals for the lifestyle you desire, and your ideas and dreams for your children into projects you fully share and supportively work on together.

Prenuptial agreements open a tricky field of discussion. Many brides and grooms think that nothing could be more unromantic. When we asked friends of ours, Art Klein and Pat Feinman, if they had considered a prenup when they married eight years ago, they were horrified. They characterized prenups as "blasphemous."

On the other hand, for those who are wealthy, prenups can be the height of romance, as they can answer the question "Am I loved for who I am or for what I have?" If the idea of a prenup causes no distress, then odds are good that it's love that truly brings a couple together.

In the reality of today's world, marital finances — with dual incomes, pension plans, wills and estate planning, blended families, first and second mortgages, investments, and inheritance provisions — are becoming ever more complex. So, even though you might not want a legally rendered prenup, it is very wise for the two of you to develop some form of written financial understanding before you marry.

Avoiding Problems

Many couples who married young told us they never talked about money beforehand because they "were broke," "just starting out," or "never thought about it." But several admitted that their ignorance about each other's financial beliefs and spending styles created problems that later damaged their marriages. Deborah and Walter were very generous in relating their story of disaster and recovery:

> Walter and I didn't do a prenup because we felt neither of us had enough assets to even think about that. Unfortunately, we weren't very enlightened about financial planning, either. Like so many Americans, we fell into the trap of putting too much on credit cards during our five-year courtship and the beginning of our marriage. We also charged the bulk of our rather upscale wedding. Neither of us liked dealing with numbers, and the unspoken understanding was that Walter would handle paying the bills. I sure didn't want to be bothered with it.
>
> Pretty soon we began to have an inkling that we were getting into too much debt, but we fooled ourselves into thinking that was normal and "the American way." I thought of myself as very independent and bright, but when it came to finances I just wasn't thinking straight. By the time I decided to find out what was really going on (I wanted to start saving), I realized we had maxed out about a dozen cards and were almost forty thousand in debt, which was more than either of our annual salaries. It was catastrophic and eventually contributed to a ten-month separation.

By that time, we had been arguing for years, blaming each other for the mess we were in. It caused a lot of fear and bruised feelings. I was convinced that if I stayed with Walter, I'd be living in poverty because he was so bad with money. In fairness, I wasn't exactly complaining when he suggested extravagant vacations, gifts, and restaurants. My "ignorance is bliss" approach was totally irresponsible.

Happily, we salvaged our marriage and emerged even stronger, *and* we dramatically changed our spending habits. I took control of the finances (with Walter's blessing), educated myself, and devised a plan. I consolidated our debt, switched to credit cards with lower interest rates, paid them down one by one, and found corners to cut. Over the course of several years, both of our salaries increased significantly, so we were able to dig out.

I am very proud to say we owe zero on credit cards now. We own a beautiful townhome in Marina del Rey, California. We even have some savings. None of that would have happened if I had kept my head in the sand or if we hadn't both decided to work out the issues. It was quite a learning process for us, one that nearly destroyed our relationship. But deciding to take control of our finances made our marriage stronger, more trustworthy, and lots more fun.

I realize now that some financial planning could have helped us avoid years of horrible stress and tension. Live and learn.

Learning to Live in Financial Truth

So that the two of you won't have to live and learn, you can, at minimum, create your own agreement outlining how you will handle money and finances in your marriage. Below are basic mandatory financial questions for every couple, no matter their financial situation. Use this list to both stimulate and guide your discussions.

❖ *What assets and debts will each of you bring to your marriage?*

❖ *Will one or both of you work?*

❖ *What are your current annual pretax incomes?*

❖ *What preliminary budget will you use during the first year of married life to track your expenses?*

❖ *Will one or both of you pay bills, reconcile bankbooks, handle tax and financial records, and otherwise manage money?*

❖ *Will you establish a monthly review session to bring yourselves up to date on your assets and debts? If not, why?*

❖ *What is your plan for monthly savings?*

❖ *What is your plan for paying off any debts?*

❖ *What need do you have for the money you might receive as wedding gifts?*

❖ *Do either of you need further schooling to create the life you want together? If so, what will it cost?*

❖ *Do you plan to own your own home?*

❖ *How do you plan to pay for the education of your children (if you choose to have any)?*

❖ *What are your goals for investing and for retirement?*

❖ *How do you plan to learn more about wise investing?*

❖ *Will you want to travel? If so, how will you finance it?*

❖ *When will you have your will drawn up?*

❖ *Are there other matters you need to clarify? Discuss expected inheritances, the terms of any spousal and/or child support agreements, any gambling that either of you might do, and so forth.*

If one or both of you cannot bring yourselves to jointly answer the above questions (and other questions that come to mind), you might consider whether you are prepared for the adult responsibilities of marriage, which include taking your financial relationship seriously.

Our society is strange in that we can more easily talk about our sex lives than ask others how much money they make. That's why a sincere and open discussion about each partner's individual finances not only can be but — we guarantee it — *will* be as intimate an exchange as you will ever have. And yes, it will be romantic, too, because you will share yourselves with each other in ways that require courage and surrender.

Later in this chapter, we provide guidelines for discussing and negotiating all the financial questions above as well as others that might arise. These guidelines will help you to open the door to ongoing financial planning, which is part of real-life love and real-life romance. If you avoid it, real love will take a back-seat to ignorance or self-indulgence, and that is the road to disaster.

Our Creative Agreement

We agreed to create a prenup before we married. Judith bought an hour with an attorney to learn what developing the agreement would involve. The attorney said that the best way to negotiate a prenup was to behave as though we were preparing for divorce: each of us should hire our own attorney and then hammer out the agreement. "But we're not even married yet," Judith protested, leaving before the hour was up.

With a bit more research, we learned that we could draw up our own agreement and have a family law attorney review it, which we did. She helped us to clarify several issues and simplified some of our wording. She was a delight, congratulating us on creating positive insurance against later financial problems.

After we had changed the document according to her suggestions, we had it notarized and filed it with the county clerk. That was it. One hour of our attorney's time and seventeen dollars for the county clerk's office, and we had what we wanted.

In retrospect, we realize that we should have included our goals for the future in our agreement. But those conversations arose in due time. So, that was the financial aspect of our agreement. Emotionally and spiritually, the evening we spent discussing the details was one of the most intimate evenings of our early life together. We trusted each other with the facts of our individual finances: the incomes we each earned, the debts we had, the savings we'd accumulated, our individual spending styles, our goals for how we wanted to live, and our thoughts about the finances we'd need to make that life possible. What could be more romantic than our honest desire to be completely open and willing to accept each other as we really were?

A Formal Prenuptial Agreement

If either of you has considerable means, we strongly advise you to draw up a legal prenuptial agreement. If you are the one with the assets and your future spouse fights you on this, please consider whether you want to marry someone who objects to clarifying and protecting the assets you have accumulated prior to your marriage.

Dee Dee and Hank, who each brought considerable assets to their union and recently married in New York City, both knew they wanted a prenup. But, as Dee Dee said, "Dealing with the attorneys was far more complicated than we'd imagined, and we should have left more time to think through all the issues." Yet it was Hank who was most impressed by the process. "It forced us to open up and talk about touchy issues. We even talked about our will and what we would want for our children if, God forbid, we both passed away when they were young, topics we'd never have touched otherwise."

Frederick, a licensed independent minister, is married to Joan. They are an interracial couple — he is African American, she's Caucasian. They wrote their entire wedding ceremony and held it in a lovely setting at Joan's son's home. Frederick, who is also a cook, personally catered the reception. They also created a prenup. As he tells it, they were "faith-guarding her investments. She lost a lot in her previous marriage, so she was understandably anxious. But I was not marrying her property; I was marrying a woman I love dearly."

Rather than a battle-oriented attorney like the one Judith encountered, Frederick and Joan found an attorney who helped them work out the details. The agreement spelled out that everything each of them had accumulated prior to their marriage would remain that partner's sole property and that everything acquired after the wedding would be joint property. A specific point was made about the condo they now live in, which belongs to Joan. The agreement states that should Joan die first, Frederick can live in the condo until it's his time to leave the earth. Only then would it formally pass to Joan's children.

As Frederick said, "What's behind the desire for a prenup is often concern for children in the event of sickness or death. It's a terrific way to clarify how the two of you want things to proceed when you are calm and able to think clearly, rather than later, when emotional chaos might be overwhelming.

"In my relationship with Joan, I have never felt entitled. I treasure its real value, which is our emotional and spiritual life."

Anything Goes

Barb and Nick, who had both been married before, spent quite a long time talking about their finances during the first few months of being together. As Nick put it:

> The conversations were often painful for me, as I had ideas about who a man is "supposed" to be financially that conflicted with who I was at the time. What I came to was that I had a choice. I could get past my limiting conversation about men's roles and women's roles and deal on the basis of what works for us, or I could be right about the roles and doom our relationship.
>
> Since those opening conversations, we have had many more, and they exist in the context of our intention to have this relationship serve us both as individuals and as us. Even though Barb consulted a friend of hers, an attorney, who gave her a document to use as a template, we wrote up our financial agreement according to our own specific needs, signing it within the first year we were together. This was just part of a larger agreement that covers many areas of our life together, and we are more than pleased to say that it's working.

While Barb and Nick felt no need to formally involve an attorney, Elisabeth Posner Schouten and Peter Schouten avoided legal involvement altogether. Elisabeth had been married once before, and Peter had signed divorce papers twice. This time, they didn't want to take any risks. So they prepared their own homemade document to clarify how they would handle their finances and protect their individual assets.

The Schoutens won the 1999 *Washington Post*–sponsored "Honey, I Need Some Money" contest. Michelle Singletary, who writes the *Post's* "The Color of Money" column, says the thing about the Schoutens' prenuptial agreement that "tickled" her was the stipulation, championed by Elisabeth, that they "would have to go out to dinner at least once a week."

When it comes to your personal financial agreements, anything goes. For Elisabeth, building in certain entertainment expenses was important. You could include a requirement to spend a certain amount on health and fitness, or on support for your parents in their older years. Be pragmatic *and* romantic! It's your agreement, so write it up to delineate and protect all that you consider important, most especially your relationship with each other.

Your Productive Money Discussions

You might be tempted to avoid money discussions and financial planning, afraid that you'll open up a can of worms, upset the apple cart, scare your partner, or get in a lather over nothing. Yet you're far better off tackling financial matters and money-related issues now rather than later, when you might have built up a poor track record, to say nothing of resentments.

Talking about money can be more intimate than having sex, and when you observe the following guidelines, you will emerge from your conversations feeling far more connected and safe with each other. Remember throughout this process that you love each other and that you need to feel financially safe in your relationship.

❖ *Review the "Learning to Live in Financial Truth" questions above.*

❖ *Answer each question in turn so that neither of you has to lead or follow all the time.*

❖ *Do not criticize or make fun of your partner's answers — no matter how odd they might seem to you.*

❖ *Ask questions about your partner's answers if you need further clarification, but do not belittle your partner or express contempt in any way.*

❖ *Keep track of those issues which you automatically agree upon (or nearly agree) and those that reveal challenging differences.*

❖ *Now return to the topics which you differed upon. These need further exploration so that you can reconcile them to both of your satisfaction.*

❖ *For each such issue, take turns explaining — from the deepest level of your fears, concerns, family histories, and desires — the emotional reasons that you feel the way you do. There can be no debate about these explanations because you are expressing feelings, not facts. Practice respecting each other's point of view. Some of your disagreements might be resolved simply by understanding each other more intimately.*

❖ *Now, for each unresolved issue, you can both offer ideas that you've not previously considered but would satisfy your needs. Nothing is too wild, too extreme, or too petty. But don't attack your lover's suggestions.*

❖ *Keep this loving, creative think tank going until you find a resolution for each issue. And, if this takes more than one conversation, that's not a problem unless one or both of you is off track — determined to have it your way and only your way. If that's the case, beware. You are no longer in a relationship of two; you're only in a relationship with yourself.*

❖ *Celebrate yourselves! You are the authors of a unique, thoughtfully considered financial agreement, whether you now take it to an attorney or stick it on the refrigerator with a magnet. Either way, you have taken your love seriously, and that's a serious success.*

You Know You're Spiritually and Financially Rich When...

As a child, you might not have been taught to be smart about money, much less the ins and outs of wise investing. So here's a checklist of smart money behaviors that we wish we'd learned earlier in our lives. Answer "true" or "false" to each of the following statements, then discuss your answers and examine your current attitudes and actions with your partner.

❖ *You pay your bills on time.*

❖ *Before you make any major purchase or investment, you seek advice from an accountant and/or someone wise in the ways of money.*

❖ *Shopping is not your solution for depression or even your idea of a great hobby.*

❖ *You look for bargains, enjoy purchasing items on sale, and don't hesitate to try to negotiate better deals when possible.*

❖ *It is your practice to continually learn how to save and invest your money.*

❖ *Each month you put some of your earnings into a savings account or an investment.*

❖ *Taking a loss on investments doesn't embarrass you, and when necessary you get out of them rather than fantasize that they'll come around.*

❖ *You go to seminars and/or take classes that expand your understanding of tax planning and investment options.*

❖ *You always have a good sense of your credit card balance and generally pay off your card(s) at the end of each month.*

❖ *You enjoy using a credit card that earns you frequent-flier miles, and you put your phone bill, cable bill, and any other recurring bills on that card whenever possible.*

❖ *You take advantage of and use credit cards with zero percent interest when your cash flow is tight, and you never falter in making your payments on time.*

❖ *You purchase only the types of insurance that you actually need and that are appropriate for your situation.*

❖ *You have an eye on retirement even now, and always make the maximum contribution to your pension or retirement fund.*

❖ *If you own your home, you've looked into refinancing and/or an equity line of credit based on the value of your property in order to maximize your use of assets.*

❖ *You realize that real estate offers various opportunities for good investment.*

❖ *You want your money to work for you so you won't have to work for money all your life.*

❖ *You really get a kick out of watching your money grow.*

We've included these statements because we were both ignorant about financial matters, including investment, earlier in our lives. Talking through these points can show you your own possibilities, if you're willing to set your intentions and learn about financial planning together.

Give yourselves the best wedding present possible: establish the foundation for a secure financial future. As we learned seventeen years ago when we chose to develop our own prenup, consciously building that foundation can be among the most intimate, romantic projects of a couple's life.

CHAPTER 9

The Power of Your Vows

We were so pleased that our minister suggested we write our own vows. It helped us realize that she had faith in our maturity, and it was so touching to say what we felt and believed rather than repeat something impersonal.

— Kerry Sato, translator, District of Columbia

Your wedding vows are the doorway to your future, to a loving adventure that will never stop unfolding. They are the public announcement of your commitment to each other and a statement of your beliefs. They establish the character of your marriage and are a pledge to let go of old ways that are no longer appropriate so that you'll be free to follow wherever love leads. Your vows are a foundation you can rely upon as you grow and change in your new, emerging life.

Last year, dear friends of ours gave these vows to each other:

GARY: I, Gary Mark Goldberg, choose you, Joan Mary Wegman, in front of our friends, family, and children, to be my life partner from this day forward. I promise to sleep by your side, to be the joy of your heart and the food of your soul, and to be the best person I can be for you. I promise to laugh with you when times are good and to suffer with you when they are bad. I promise to wash away your tears with my kisses and to hold you sweetly and gladly until our days on earth are over.

In pledge of my commitment, I give you this ring. Wear it always and know that I love you more than life itself and will always be here for you.

JOAN: I, Joan Mary Wegman, proudly choose you, Gary Mark Goldberg, in front of our friends, family, and children, to be my life partner from this day forward. I promise to give you the best of myself and to love you always. I promise to hold you close when you need to be held, to laugh with you when you laugh, and, as our bodies grow old, I promise to love you even more. From this moment on, may our sunshine be shared, our rains gentle, and our love eternal. And when our days are over, may we stand by each other's side with as much love as we have today.

In pledge of this commitment, I give you this ring. As you wear it, think of this day and how much I love you, wanting only the best for you and happiness in our love.

More and more often, couples are speaking their own words as they take the journey from twoness into oneness, blessing their intent with the magic of their differences and giving way to the love and tenderness that bind them together.

Oops

What if you haven't thought about creating your own vows? After you read what Amy wrote to ultimatewedding.com, you might want to consider doing so. Amy describes what happened during her friend's wedding ceremony when the bride and groom chose to repeat vows they had not themselves written.

"During the vow exchange the preacher turned to the groom and said, 'Do you take this woman to be your *awful* wife?' Very upset, the preacher corrected himself, saying, 'To be your *lawful* wife?' By this time we were snickering, much to the bride's family's dismay. And then the kicker: the groom repeated it word for word — 'I take this woman to be my *awful lawful* wife.' If I hadn't been a bridesmaid, I would have died laughing!"

This groom, and many others like him, deserves our compassion. No doubt he was anxious and in a bit of a daze. Not wanting to make a mistake, he fell into sheer and utter obedience, resulting in an embarrassingly unconscious moment.

When your vows are not personal, when they do not reflect how each of you feel about the relationship that is specific to the two of you, they cannot touch your soul and will have little authority to guide you as a couple through your rite of passage as well as in years to come.

The Power of Personal Vows

In this chapter, we include several examples of couples' vows to help you become more conscious of the fact that your vows are not merely words but are also the backbone of your life as a couple, now and tomorrow.

Tina Tessina, our colleague and fellow relationship author,

shared the vows she and her husband created over twenty
years ago:

> We wrote our own wedding script for the ceremony, and
> our own vows, which were based on my husband's spir-
> itual study. We seriously renew our commitment and
> our vows every anniversary. We have a discussion first
> about how we're doing (so far it's been wonderful) and
> what we need to change, if anything; then we recommit
> with these words:
>
> "I, Richard, take thee, Tina, to be my wife [vice versa
> for me], to the mutual benefit of all, manifesting creative
> energy for happiness in the here and now and accom-
> plishment in the proper time and place. And we thank
> Thee for that which we need to know, for bringing to us
> those whom we need to meet, and for the courage to act
> upon that knowledge in easy, natural, healthy, and bal-
> anced ways."

Like many couples, they took their vows very seriously. And,
by reading them again on each anniversary, Tina and Richard
use them as an ongoing reminder of the meaning of their marriage and a guideline for living a life of purpose.

The words *love, honor, cherish, keep,* and *promise* can be found
in most traditional vows. But crucial elements of healthy loving,
such as the conscious development of trust, are conspicuously
absent. So are promises to respect each other's differences, resolve
conflicts in a healthy manner, maintain an ongoing dialogue, and
cultivate romance on a daily basis.

Some couples discuss these points, and then the partner who
is the most gifted writer prepares them. Other couples sketch
out their words together, writing and rewriting until they both

feel their words express the spiritual depth and loving essence of their union.

By writing your own vows — even if you select a few lines from a book or borrow a romantic verse from a song — the two of you will not only personalize your ceremony but, more important, affirm your marriage from the time you choose what to say. As Marsha, a young widow who plans to marry again, told us, "I think vows should represent what the couple desires — they shouldn't be standard, impersonal vows. Why have an impersonal wedding?"

Judith and Jim's Vows

As we prepared for our wedding, we discussed the most significant elements that we wanted to include in our vows. Then we split up those topics according to which meant the most to each of us, and then we each wrote five short vows: four individual vows, plus one that we would speak together. Below are one vow by each of us and the one we said together to close our vows.

JIM: I offer to you my vow of commitment
I promise to stand with you
and build a future
to which I commit my energies and dreams
my most closely held treasures
my just plain everyday self
all of who I am.
I commit to bring to our life together
my spirit
my soul
my feelings
my thoughts
my words

my body
and my pledge of love.

JUDITH: I accept this vow you offer to me and return it to you in kind.

JUDITH: I offer to you my vow of honor and respect
for the ways that you are different from me.
It is easy to think your ways are wrong and mine are right.

It requires my love to remember that your ways are foreign rather than wrong.

My experience with you already teaches me that we can negotiate resolutions when I see you as being just as right as I am.

And I can learn from you because sometimes your ways are "more right" than mine.

JIM: I accept this vow you offer to me and return it to you in kind.

JUDITH AND JIM: Now I acknowledge our humanness. I know that neither of us will be able to live up to the vows we have just made to each other without faltering. Therefore, my final vow to you is that I will respect your intentions, trust your sincerity, and commit my love to you today and for the remainder of our lives.

In the vows we didn't include here, we promised never to leave during a conflict, to hold each other in support and esteem, and to honor that part of us that is childlike and sensitive to being emotionally hurt. We affirmed our courage to face the challenges of married life, which we knew would be necessary to transform us.

Because we both come from families that had great difficulty valuing our individuality, it was important that the magic of our differences and our human frailty be central themes in our vows.

Beth and Mark's Vows

MARK: Elizabeth, I vow to cherish your body, your mind, and your Spirit and to nurture you in times of need. I pledge to you my respect, my faith, and my utmost trust in you, so that your freedom may never be challenged or weakened. I promise to encourage your creative expressions and to support you in your ventures apart from me. Most of all, I declare my undying love for you and make you this promise: to be a loyal and true friend, to the very best of my abilities, for as long as I live.

BETH: Mark, I vow to stand as a witness to the evolution of your soul and as a guardian of your solitude, so that you may become ever more true to yourself. I take you to be my husband in equal love as a mirror for my true Self, as a partner on my path, as your friend and lover. I vow to continue opening my heart, surrendering my fears, and bringing my love to all situations we encounter, so that through love we may grow deeper in love together. I vow to respect and celebrate the magnificence that is you, in sorrow and in joy, until death do us part.

Beth and Mark, each in their own way, share primary values in their love: the uplifting of each other and the magnificence of continued personal growth.

Pat and Art's Vows

Pat and Art, who are Jewish, were married by a gay Episcopalian minister. Through their choice of officiant, they expressed their commitment to cherish the beauty of differences.

After the minister had blessed them with wise, poetic words, he took them through the standard "Will you/I will" vows. Then he turned to their assembled community and asked, "Will all of you witnessing these promises do everything in your power to love and support Patricia and Art in their marriage?" Their friends and family vowed, "We will!"

Then Pat and Art exchanged their own vows:

PAT AND ART: I take you as my [wife/husband],
[Patricia/Art],
To have and hold you,
To honor you, to treasure you,
To be at your side in sorrow and in joy,
And to love and cherish you always.
This is my joyous and irrevocable vow.

Then they exchanged rings:

PAT AND ART: I give you this ring as a symbol of my vow, and with all that I have, all that I am, and all that I shall become, I honor you, in the name of all life and creation.

Art and Pat chose words that echoed fairly traditional vows, but they made them their own. They limited the length of their vows, and they chose to both say the same things. No matter the vows' length or style, there is a sacred power in two people naming, on their own terms, the values and ideals they pledge to uphold. And their minister involved everyone in the vows, drawing the circle of community around Pat and Art at the very moment they officially stepped into their new life.

Love Letters as Part of Your Vows

If you prefer traditional vows but still want to include something personal that will accentuate the intimacy and individuality of the moment, you may want to write love letters to each other that would be included during your ceremony.

"The Catholic priest who married us," Nicole wrote, "was very close to Ben. He asked us to write each other a love letter a few days before our wedding. Since he didn't know me all that well, he wanted to read them to get a sense of us as a couple. We shared our hopes, our fears, what we loved about each other, and we expressed our commitment to a life together.

"During the ceremony, as the priest was about to give his homily about marriage, he pulled out the letters (much to my horror since it was such a personal letter and I felt terribly exposed). He explained to our family and friends why he'd asked us to write them. He told me not to worry — he was only going to read a few parts of the letters so that everyone gathered in support of our union would hear how we felt. As he read them, Ben and I clung to each other and cried. So did many of our guests.

"It's almost nine years later and the one memory I treasure most from our wedding day is those two letters.

I expected that we'd look at the photos and the video, and occasionally we do. But the one thing we always do on our anniversary is reread the letters, and we still cry.

"When couples ask for wedding advice, I always recommend writing a heartfelt letter days before the ceremony, if only to give to each other as your wedding gift. It is a wonderful reminder of the truly blissful expectations and the frailties of joining with another."

Now It's Your Turn

If you haven't already written your vows, you might want to answer and discuss the following questions together:

❖ *What does this marriage mean to you — to each of you?*
❖ *What are you truly vowing to do and to be in your marriage?*

Now complete the following sentences. Your answers might please you so much that you'll want to include these sentences in your vows. Or they might simply help you get started.

❖ *I love you because...*
❖ *I will be true to this relationship because...*
❖ *I will honor you as different from me because...*

We suggest that you also include some version of these two fundamental concepts in your vows:

❖ *I will forgive you, and myself, when we fall back into old patterns and mistreat each other. (It is essential that you both recognize that you will arrive into your marriage with emotional histories, pasts that will require compassion at times. If you don't, you will repeat old patterns, unconsciously hurt each other, and possibly refuse to accept responsibility for your actions. Then the full process and meaning of joining together in marriage will be closed to you.)*

❖ *I will remember that this marriage is a spiritual and psychological workshop, a continuous healing and learning experience. (Urges to control, desires to force the other to change, and unwillingness to examine ourselves are impulses we all share. But they are contrary to the spirit of marriage. When you give in to learn more about yourselves and each other, your joy in being together will only increase.)*

Managing Stage Fright

If you anticipate being nervous, maybe even extremely nervous, keep your vows fairly brief. You can memorize them, but hide cheat sheets in the groom's pocket and beneath the bride's bouquet in case your nervousness causes a memory lapse. Or you can have your officiant guide you through the vows, as is done traditionally, only this time she or he will guide you through your own vows. Or you can read your vows to each other. If you do this, make sure to take tiny breaks from looking at your papers to look at each other. No matter the style of delivery you choose, practice ahead of time so you will be comfortable with your words and will speak loudly enough that everyone can hear you.

Make sure to keep your vows to the point. This will help you stay relatively calm because the words you speak during your service will feel right and whole. You will be carried along, supported, and buoyed up by the heartfelt emotion embodied in your words.

Quenesha and Terence, who opted for a traditional ceremony in deference to their parents, nevertheless felt it was essential to write their own vows. Quenesha memorized hers and said them word for word, barely able to hold back her tears. Terence opted for spontaneity and spoke from his heart. He too found it difficult to hold back his tears. He capped off his vows by stealing a kiss, much to the surprise of his bride, their guests, and especially the minister.

Transforming Yourselves

Vows are the centerpiece of the marriage rite, powerful, transformative messages to each other and to yourselves. It is your words that will bind you together, not the music or the prayers or even the proclamation by the officiant. When you take them seriously, they will help to make your emotional and spiritual transition profoundly real.

Whether you're planning an elaborate, expensive affair or will be married in a judge's chambers, we hope you won't miss the magic of speaking your own mind and hearing your own words as you voice the special commitment that only the two of you will share.

When Jim's brother, Bill, and his bride, Kelly, married six years ago in Hawaii, they wrote out what they wanted the minister to say as well as their own vows:

MINISTER: We have come together here today to join Bill and Kelly in their declaration to share their lives together, one with the other. They have come to this beautiful island and presented themselves in the presence of all we call Divine. There are no human ties so sweet and tender as marriage. It is a state of conscious unity in thought and purpose, in plan and action. On this day you stand somewhat apart from all other human beings, for you stand within the charmed circle of your love for each other. This love is not your possession. It is a source of energy that flows freely through each of you and gives you the courage to live your lives more fully.

We stand in the spirit of Aloha. Aloha recognizes a bonding of all people and expresses that bonding through love, affection, compassion, and kindness. Aloha acknowledges the value and worth of all people. Your desire to integrate the spirit of Aloha into the framework of a meaningful life together deserves great respect. You deserve to experience love that will continually bring you joy and make both of you better people, a love that will give you the strength to face the responsibilities of married life. And you deserve a home, a sanctuary of serenity where the values of your lives will be generated and upheld.

KELLY: Our commitment is to create and experience our love and life to their fullest potential; to develop our own unique way of sharing our lives together; to accept, support, nourish, and replenish each other in times of stress and to acknowledge, celebrate, validate, and remember all of this in times of joy; to design our own traditions and memories together, as well as with those we love; and to take time out to dance together and laugh a lot.

BILL: When we come to the end of our lives together, we will be able to say to each other, "Because you have loved me well, my heart has flown off its branch and is still hovering in the air. Because you have loved me well, I have faith in myself. Because you have loved me well, I have faith in all humanity."

MINISTER: Marriage is composed of two separate beings, each different, seeking life's fulfillment together. Today you open the doors to the endless possibilities of your future and to the opportunity for Soul to dance in your hearts.

BILL: Do you see these hands? When they move over you, they cannot encompass you; they travel the distances of your legs; they coil in the light of your waist. For me, you are a treasure more laden with immensity than the sea, and you are white and blue and spacious like the earth. In that territory, from your feet to your brow, walking, walking, walking, I shall spend my life.

KELLY: Take bread away from me, if you wish; take air away, but do not take your laughter from me. Your laughter rises to the sky and opens for me all the doors of life — it is the spring flower I was waiting for. Laugh at the night, at the day, at the moon. But when I open my eyes and close them, when my steps go and return, deny me bread, air, or spring, but never deny me your laughter.

BILL AND KELLY IN TURN (JOINING HANDS): I, [Kelly/Bill], take you, [Bill/Kelly], as my [husband/wife]. I promise to love and cherish you from this day forward. I choose you alone to be my [husband/wife]. I will comfort and honor you at all times and, forgetting all others, will remain faithful to you alone.

I give you this ring with all my heart. Let it always be to us a symbol of our love and a token of our commitment to each other.

Beyond right and wrong there is a field...let us meet there.

CHAPTER 10

Special People in Your Ceremony

Since my husband and I have children from previous marriages, we included a ceremony in which we placed a gold ring on each child's ring finger and told them that we promised to include them in our lives and our hearts forever. We did it as a surprise, and the children loved it. And there wasn't a dry eye in the church!

— Robin, usabride.com

Your wedding will be one of the most personal moments of your life. And yet what about those who will be there with you — your parents, siblings, other relatives, and friends? Have you considered involving them more personally? In many weddings, such guests, even if they are attendants or escorts, are left as mere observers. But weddings hold great potential for acknowledging and honoring those who are truly special to you.

Making Guests Feel Special

Among the best ways to ensure your guests feel deeply involved in your wedding is to address them in your ceremony — through either your officiant's words or by speaking directly to your gathering. Wedding coordinator Christine Stieber, owner of The Perfect Day (www.The-Perfect-Day.com), who sees her job as "being there for my wedding couple as well as taking care of everyone who will be at their wedding," appreciates officiants who involve the wedding party and guests by speaking to them on behalf of the couple.

Give your officiant specific and personal information so that your ceremony will weave a connection between you and your loved ones and create a conscious sense of community. Stacie and Jed provided a flavor of what their minister said on their behalf: "I want you all to know how thrilled Stacie and Jed are that Aunt Madelynne and Uncle Jerry were able to fly in all the way from Southern California. And they want to especially thank Stacie's maid of honor and only sister, Josie, who provided spiritual support and practical, day-to-day help, adding a very deep richness to Stacie and Jed's special day."

Bo Yerxa, a justice of the peace who has married more than 120 couples, told us that he and his wife, participants in the post-sixties alternative movement, had lived communally with other people. Their lifestyle included various collective and cooperative activities, including the purchase of nearly a thousand acres of cooperatively held land in Maine on which individual households built cabins. As he told us:

> This arrangement and the associated web of relationships led to considerable shared parenting. When my daughter, Shyla Bliss Yerxa, and her husband, Gabriel Lowery, were

married a couple of years ago, I performed the wedding. The three of us wrote a passage that I delivered: "Shyla and Gabe have asked me to say a few words to express their gratitude to the many among you who have supported them into adulthood. All of you — family and friends — have played important, caring roles in their lives, providing love and laughter. They extend their love to each of you and are honored that you are here to share in their happiness."

Tina Tessina involved everyone at her wedding by having "the entire congregation hold hands during the prayer in which the congregation pledged to support the couple and Richard and I took communion. The minister had previously cut the bread into a heart shape, which was greeted with cheering and applause when he held it up for everyone to see."

Christine Stieber has seen officiants, prior to starting the official ceremony, ask all the married couples present to think back to their own wedding days — their own excitement and love — which infuses a great spirit of involvement among the guests. "Inevitably," Christine said, "most couples hold hands or lean into each other or touch their heads together. It brings everyone closer. Even the singles can feel the loving, open-hearted spirit move through the crowd and bring them all together for the couple."

If you prefer to express your appreciation yourselves, as we did, speak directly to several people at your gathering and describe the specific reasons why their presence is so significant. Of course, it won't be possible to address each person. So let everyone know that they were invited because they are important to you, and that you are grateful to have each and every one of them with you on your special day.

Considering Your Attendants

When planning her first wedding, Janie, who comes from a large Italian family, just copied what she'd seen all her cousins do. "Looking back, I wouldn't have had such a large bridal party. I had ten bridesmaids and ten groomsmen, two flower girls, and the ring bearer. Twenty-three people I had to organize, direct, and control. And they all delayed paying me what they owed for their dresses and tuxedos. Constantly reminding them was a nightmare."

After her divorce, she met Tony. While planning their wedding, she said, "This time, we're having only our two closest friends, and they get to wear their own clothes. I have to approve, of course. But it saves them money, and it saves my sanity."

Tony added, "And they're not just going to stand there. We've asked them to prepare something they will say just before we take our vows about how they experience us together. We don't want them to be window dressing. We want the blessing of their care for us."

How might you redesign your wedding party's participation? Traditionally, wedding parties have just looked alike. They filed in, and stood there. Is that enough for you and for them? Perhaps, several weeks before your wedding, you could gather everyone together (those who are out of town can connect by phone) and collectively come up with ideas that would be especially touching and appropriate for who you are and who they are. Do this well in advance so everyone can be fully prepared by the time of your wedding.

It's also helpful to consider whether you really want your attendants to dress identically. We talked with many bridesmaids who complained that they had had to pay upward of $400 for their dresses, $125 for shoes, and another $100 to $250 for hairdressers, manicure, and hosiery. "And for what?" said one. "Just to stand there." One mother told us that her twenty-nine-year-old daughter "has been invited to be a bridesmaid so many times she's already had to spend almost twenty thousand dollars to pay for the apparel, parties, and wedding gifts. And she's far from rich."

In earlier times, the wedding party dressed just like the wedding couple because it was thought that happiness enraged demonic forces. The passage into marriage was a fragile, transitional time of intense peril when the wedding couple was vulnerable to being snatched away. Disguising the wedding party in identical clothes was a way to fool the diabolical phantoms that were thought to lurk nearby. Although we might no longer believe in evil spirits, the tradition continues in the coordinated attire of ushers and bridesmaids.

It's supposed to be an honor to be asked to pay for one's wardrobe when standing up for friends at a wedding. But let's reconsider this burden. After all, your wedding party will do a great deal to help you before and during your wedding day. You can lighten their load, and make your wedding more personal and creative, by choosing not to saddle them with the expense of clothing they might not like or use again.

If you can afford it, feel free to include as many attendants in your wedding party as you wish and to dress them in whatever way you want. But take responsibility for your choice by paying for their wardrobe. If their wardrobe must complement your decor and theme, you should be willing to pay for what you want.

If you can't afford to dress your bridesmaids and ushers but still want a specific look, consider the following possibilities:

TINA TESSINA: "I asked my bridesmaids to wear long pastel
    dresses they already had, and they all turned up in

shades of lavender! I never asked if they had planned it, but it was lovely."

CHRIS MARGOCS: "My bridesmaids lived in four different cities and had four very different bodies, so instead of a cookie-cutter bridesmaid dress, I sent them all a swatch of green fabric (for our Christmastime wedding) and asked them to find tea-length dresses that covered their shoulders and complemented their own shapes. They looked great and didn't have to spend according to my taste or budget or settle for a dress they'd never wear again."

MARTI SEIDEL-CLARK: "When I was maid of honor for my best friend in college, three of us bridesmaids found a reasonably priced, Victorian-style ivory blouse that we all liked and would wear again. The bride's sister made long dusty-rose skirts and cummerbunds of darker rose and forest green, and we only had to pay for the fabric. The bride gave us pink rosebuds to work into our hair any way we wanted, and we all looked great."

Labors of Love

The vendors you'll hire to cater and provide flowers, music, and refreshments will be caring and creative. That's their job, and you'll pay them for it. But have you considered the loving generosity that might be available if you also accept help from your friends? If that thought makes you squeamish, think again. The following couples opened themselves to what their friends offered and discovered precious gifts of care and effort.

Sandy and Dan's neighbor gifted them by using flowers from

her spring garden to decorate the church and to create long be-ribboned bouquets for the bride and her four bridesmaids, bou-tonnieres for the groom and his groomsmen, and corsages for the mothers and grandmothers.

Tina Tessina said, "My gown was made by my 'Best Woman' (she wanted to be called that, and my husband's friend asked to be called 'Male of Honor'). The Male of Honor was a caterer, so he made us a German chocolate wedding cake, three tiers, dec-orated with fresh daisies. I had flowers in my hair, which was coifed by a friend who is a hairdresser."

Cynthia Brian's groom, Brian Sheaff, played in a rock band. Placed at the altar, Brian's band played all the music for the cere-mony. Patty, Brian's sister, sang the solos. As Cynthia and her husband said in their program: "Music in song is the expression of our joys, fears, wants, and love. These are some of our favorites, and we hope they will have as much meaning for you as they have for us." The song list included "You Are the Sun-shine of My Life" by Stevie Wonder and "Just You and Me" by Chicago. Patty sang "Ave Maria" a cappella. The music and songs were intertwined with prayers, readings, vows, and the Mass.

When Ping Ho and Loren Bloch were married, their "friends presided over [our] wedding, provided the music throughout the day, brought the food, arranged the food tables, and took the photos. We were surrounded by such great love!"

We're not suggesting that you use your friends' help to save money, though that might be important to you, but so that you can receive the grace and love available through their help. Rather than just purchasing everything for the pleasure of your guests, you can expand your ability to tell people what you need and how they can give to you.

Open yourselves to receive the love that wants to come your way in the form of help from family and friends — creative and thoughtful care that you might otherwise turn away or take for granted.

Honoring Those Who Are Gone

Many couples feel strongly about including parents, grand-parents, and even siblings who did not live long enough to be present at the wedding.

Liliana and Jackson placed eight-by-ten framed photographs of her grandparents and his father on a table beside the riser in the San Francisco hotel ballroom where they took their vows. Flowers surrounded the photographs, and a banner made by a calligrapher graced the table: "You are forever in our hearts. We love you! Liliana and Jackson."

Julia's father passed away the February before she and Jeffrey were married. As she told us, "My father was a wonderful piano player. During the later part of his sickness, he taped himself playing Bach, Beethoven, and Mozart. Right before Jeffrey and I were married, I received a copy. During our lighting of the unity candle, we played my father's tape. It was as if he were right there with us. His music filled the church and filled my heart and soul with his beauty. It was perfect, a moment I will never forget."

Judy Collier Lynne shared, "When my daughter Kim married two months ago, just a year after both of my parents — who she was extremely close to — had passed away, she asked me to carry my dad's Bible and put it on the chair next to me. She asked my sister to carry one of my mom's little teddy bears (she collected them) and put it on the chair next to her. So in the front row we had Kim's stepfather, Mike; me; my dad's Bible; my mom's teddy bear; my sister; and her husband. It was very special."

Including Readers, Soloists, and Blessings

Whether you want friends to read poetry or passages from the Bible, Kahlil Gibran, or other wisdom teachings, or whether you want singers or instrumentalists to honor you with their musical gifts, be sure to incorporate these participants into the proceedings in a manner that extends the beauty of your ceremony and echoes the intimacy you are creating through your love. As Chris Margocs told us:

> Ed and I are Catholic and attended premarriage sessions with a married couple who were our "engaged sponsors." They took us through a curriculum that covered all aspects of the married relationship. This requirement of the church, as well as the six-month preparatory time and interview by the priest, really helped us solidify our intention to get married and stay married.
>
> They also helped us realize how in tune we were with each other and our vision of the future and made us feel more confident about our relationship. That's why we asked our sponsors to be readers in our ceremony, which honored and emphasized their role in our marital preparations.

We were deeply touched when our friends Beth and Mark invited us to give a final blessing before their recessional. We offered the following words:

> Beth and Mark, let the marriage you have vowed to live intoxicate you with the miracle of who you are. Open to the goodness that exists in each of you, no matter what form or shape it may take. Don't forget to leave room in your heart to embrace the lessons of the darker side as

well. Surrender to the force that moves you to care, to feel compassion, to say over and over that the one you love is so very, very special.

When you do this, then love whispers, let me come to you and I will. When you let me come to you, I promise I will be there with you in challenge and in joy, always leading you to an ever closer, more intimate relationship grounded in the depth and richness of who each of you really is.

Real romance always arises from the stillpoint at the center of what you cocreate together, and that is the meaning of marriage and the spiritual purpose for which you have joined your lives.

We are honored to bless this marriage and all of you who have brought your love and support for these two very special people.

And now let us take a moment to shine our joined beam of love upon Mark and Beth. In silence, simply send what is in your hearts through your eyes and smiles into their eyes and hearts and souls. [Moment of silence.]

We love you, Beth and Mark, and we rejoice in your choice of each other!

We made a point of asking Beth and Mark to look into the eyes of their loving guests so they could consciously receive their very real support and care.

Blessed by Your Parents' Vows

You are beginning a new family, which means that, to some degree, you are leaving the family that raised you. For your new family to grow in its own right, it is best that your parents acknowledge the sanctity and privacy of your new marriage and relinquish their place at the center of your life.

However, this is a time of transition and transformation for your parents as well as for you — or it should be. Yet, in many cases, parents have a very difficult adjustment. Rather than taking for granted that they will adjust, why not acknowledge them at this time when their roles are being redefined?

Your ceremony will take on an even richer dimension when you invite all your parents, including stepparents and even grandparents, to come forward so that each can publicly establish their new position in your life and be supported in responsibly and lovingly going through their own rite of passage.

During Jennifer and Matt's ceremony, Jennifer asked her mother, Patricia, and her maternal grandmother, Doris, to join her. At one point Patricia turned to Jennifer and said, "I remember all too well the time my mother dropped in on us unannounced, just to visit. She walked in the back door just as Henry and I were..." Patricia took her mother's hand and smiled. "Well, Mom, this isn't the right place to talk about what Henry and I were doing that Saturday afternoon, is it?" As the guests chuckled warmly, Patricia turned to Jennifer and Matt and said, "I vow to never give you two any reason to have to change *your* locks."

At another woman's wedding, her grandfather said, "I'll still enjoy those cakes of yours. But I'll know now not to just call up and order one like I used to when you were a little girl." The bride welled up with tears, understanding the deep love that her grandpa could express only in his way.

You can also ask for vows that express your parents' understanding that you no longer need to be parented, or anything else specific to your situation. And, by all means, thank each of your parents for his or her generosity of spirit.

Involving Your Children in the Ceremony

If your marriage is not the first for one or both of you and there are children to be integrated or blended into your new family, consider involving your children in your ceremony. It is important, sometimes crucial, that children know they are part of the wedding vows as they transition into their new family roles.

Lakisha brought her daughters — Myllanee, five, and Kitanna, four — into her new relationship with Greg, who brought his three-year-old son, Zach. At their wedding, Lakisha wanted them to "jump the broom," a tradition that was part of her African-American heritage. Although unfamiliar to Greg, he agreed. Normally, only the bride and groom jump the broom, which symbolizes the jump from their individual pasts into their mutual future as well as jointly demonstrating loyalty, strength, and love. Lakisha and Greg invited their children to jump the broom with them, explaining to everyone present what the ritual meant and using it as an opportunity to joyously authenticate the children's entry into their new family.

Reverend Marcia Dale Lopez, a nondenominational minister, officiated at the wedding of two singer-songwriters who sang, a cappella, their entire ceremony, which they had composed together. Their four children hummed background harmony, except between their parents' several vows, when they sang backup, harmonizing on one line, "Love, love, love, sweet love."

Judy Collier Lynne told us how, at her own wedding, her daughters helped to create the unique processional:

> We were married in a rectangular garden with a lily pond in the middle. I have two adult daughters from a previous marriage who adore my new husband, Mike, so

we thought it would be very special if my daughters gave us to each other.

First, an usher escorted my dad to a spot near the altar, and another escorted my mom to join him. Then, from one side, my daughter Kim escorted Mike to a spot near the lily pond in line with the altar, and from the other side, my daughter Trisha escorted me to where Mike and Kim were standing. Kim and Trisha joined our hands and then they walked to the altar.

Mike and I stood, hands joined together, while our vocalist sang "The First Time Ever I Saw Your Face." We then walked to the altar to be married. It was so beautifully significant that there was no long walk down an aisle — we each came the same distance to each other — and that it was Kim and Trisha who gave us to each other.

Remember to Protect Yourselves

It's so easy to get caught up wanting to include everyone, especially because your wedding journey is a very emotional time. If this happens, you might fail to protect yourselves from those who would try to take over your wedding by imposing their desires on you. As a female wedding DJ complained to us, "Family and friends can make the couple miserable with emotional blackmail."

Cynthia told us how she had to lay down the law: "Two days before the wedding, the mother of our three-year-old flower girl decided that she didn't like her daughter's dress (which matched the bridesmaids'). Our colors were lavender, rose, and aqua. Since she wanted her daughter to stand out, she bought her a bright-red froufrou dress, which of course didn't fit in at all. I told her if she insisted on the red dress, then her daughter would just be a guest. The little girl wore the original gown, and she looked fabulous."

Should this kind of thing occur, no matter who might try to invade your rightful privacy, remember that self-love requires you to do what is necessary to ensure you don't allow yourselves to be mistreated. Since your wedding will be the official start of your marital relationship with family and friends, be sure to establish that relationship on firm ground — ground that, first and foremost, will support the two of you.

You might even want to practice repeating a few choice lines so that you won't be caught off guard if someone attempts to take over. Say these aloud and see how they feel:

❖ *Sorry, but that's not what we have in mind. Thanks anyway.*

❖ *No, we don't want to reconsider. We know exactly how we want to proceed.*

❖ *I need you to understand that we're creating our wedding in our own way, and we're not inviting anyone's input.*

❖ *I know that's what worked for you in your wedding, but I'm not you, and I'm doing it my way.*

❖ *Please don't take offense, but I've already told you that we're not open to your suggestions. Now please support us in what we're doing.*

❖ *If you insist on bugging me about this, I will have to refrain from speaking with you until after the wedding.*

Whatever you say, make sure you do not attack the other person; merely draw a line that bars them from further intrusion. Also, you are under no obligation to involve relatives or friends in your wedding — even if they offer or even if that is what your mom wants. Your wedding is for you, and it needs to incorporate only what will make the two of you feel honored and loved for who you really are by all who value the magic of your particular similarities and differences.

Her Beloved Aunt Ann

Sometimes, what makes a wedding special is the person who marries the couple. Eileen Ehlers, a marriage preparation and enrichment teacher, wrote to tell us about a wedding she'd just attended:

> Not since my own marriage have I been so delighted and moved by a wedding. The bride and groom, Bethanie and Jeremy, were in their early twenties. With the help of the bride's Aunt Ann, who Bethanie was very close to, they planned a wedding of simplicity and intimacy.
>
> Since they shared no church affiliation, Ann was asked to perform the ceremony. Ann applied for and was granted authorization from the Massachusetts governor's office to officiate the exchange of vows. The only requirement was that she include the vows that ask the couple to say, "I do."
>
> For their setting, Bethanie and Jeremy selected a spot in the local town park, under a spreading red oak tree near a fountain. On the arm of her younger brother, and to the music of Norah Jones's "Come Away with Me," the bride was presented to her groom. They spoke the vows they had written to pledge their love and future.
>
> Then Bethanie's mother, carrying a long lilac satin ribbon, and Jeremy's father, carrying a ribbon of ivory,

walked from opposite sides to meet in front of the young couple. The bride's mother tied the ribbons together and then, in the ancient Celtic ceremony called handfasting, she linked the couple's hands and draped them with the satin ribbons, which fluttered in the breeze.

With tears of joy and pride, Ann led them through a ceremony that evoked hope, commitment, love, and family. Close friends and supportive family members alike joined together in rejoicing to see this lovely young woman and handsome young man begin a new journey. Using tiny bottles of bubble solution, we blew hundreds of sparkling rainbow orbs that lifted into the treetops. After the short, sweet, intimate ceremony, we feasted on food and laughter.

Driving home at the end of the day, my husband and I felt a deep and profound awe at the joy a wedding promises. Despite barriers and difficulties, a couple can create a day to honor their love, a day that draws those close to them even closer, a day that marks the passage into a life that is their own to design.

CHAPTER 11

⚭

Your Staging Says a Lot

The best thing about my wedding was that we faced the crowd. Many people complimented us on how beautiful it was to see us instead of the minister.

— Courtney, usabride.com

Whan marriage ceremonies were about social status and power more than they were about any love that might have been shared by the bride and groom, it made sense that the most prominent face during the service was that of the minister, priest, rabbi, or village elder. In fact, the more prominent a position the officiant held in his community, the more his social presence was valued. Despite the fact that it was the two young people who exchanged vows, everyone faced the officiant.

But times have changed. It's important that you consider how you'll stage the various elements of your service. Each choice will say a lot about how you relate to each other and your community and how you've decided to approach your sacred moment.

Use Your Program to Involve Everyone

How many times have you attended a wedding and wondered who the bridesmaids and groomsmen were, how the bride and groom knew the officiant, and other questions that made you feel out of the loop?

Fortunately, it's becoming more common for the wedding couple to provide a program for their wedding and reception. But rather than just using your program to list what will happen, use it to involve your guests more intimately in the events of your day. You might tell them how the two of you met, share a funny, touching story of something that happened as you were planning together, or maybe say a little about the kind of life you hope to build together. Don't wait until the reception to fill your guests in on who's who, what to expect, and other things you want them to know.

Megan, thirty-four, and Jeremy, thirty-six, had a bicoastal relationship for three years before they were able to consolidate their lives in Chicago. At a conference where we spoke, Jeremy told us, "In our program, we described our relationship with each member of the wedding party. Through short notes we'd written to each one, we shared a special memory and explained why it was so important to have them stand up with us. People were impressed that we'd been so personal. And they thanked us for explaining who everybody was."

Maurice and Shannon met in India while in the Peace Corps. Maurice was healing from a divorce, and Shannon from the loss of her husband to cancer. When they returned to the

United States they chose to study at a Buddhist monastery in upstate New York.

Feeling profoundly blessed to have found each other and rejoicing in the rich spiritual lifework they shared, they chose to express the sacred gift of love throughout their wedding, which, as students, they were allowed to hold at the monastery.

Everyone wore bright colors and removed their shoes before entering the *zendo* where the wedding would take place. As guests arrived, the bride and groom shared in giving each one a red rose. They also provided programs, which explained the elements of the ceremony: the role of the priest, chanting sutras, meditations, their personal vows, and why each guest had been invited. And they described the personal transformations they experienced by surrendering to relationship with each other. Shannon summed it up: "I found in Maurice the spiritual playmate I've never had... and I've even learned to laugh when he leaves the toilet seat up!"

When you provide programs, early arrivals will have something to read and everyone will be brought together in a common, deeper understanding of your relationship and your wedding. You'll help your guests feel comfortable as they later approach members of your wedding party, because they will know something about them.

Also, be sure to add any material that will help your guests follow along with the ceremony, as well as any instructions that might be important. Rasheeda, twenty-eight, told us, "Since my fiancé, William, is three-quarters Cherokee and grew up in that culture, we explained in our program the Native American rituals that we would be using. That way, my African-American family and everyone else could appreciate their importance and meaning." Similarly, Kim, who is Christian, and Elliot, who is Jewish, combined various religious elements in their wedding service and explained the significance of those rituals to each of them in their program. On the cover of the program Janella and Morgan created for their commitment ceremony, they simply used a delightful photograph taken of them on their first date.

Finally, many people use their programs to add information and/or instructions about their receptions. For example, our friends Beth and Mark included this information:

> *There will be no reception line.*
> *Mark and Beth will greet guests*
> *throughout the dining experience.*

There is no limit to how you might use your own program to help your guests feel more comfortable, more included, and more involved in the proceedings. Trust yourselves to find what feels right for you and your community.

Amazing Grace

For our wedding, we adapted the lyrics to "Amazing Grace" to reflect our feelings for each other and for the vows we were about to take. We sang to each other, with the church choir blending in. To ensure that our guests wouldn't feel left out, we put these lyrics in our program:

> *Amazing Grace, how sweet thou ar't*
> *To touch the soul in me*
> *To quicken deep within my heart*
> *A love that set me free.*

> *Throughout this time of trials and joys*
> *A distance we have come*
> *To stand together each resolved*
> *To join our lives as one.*

> *When we've been wed full fifty years*
> *Our lives yet blessed by Grace*
> *We'll no less sing our wedding song*
> *Then when we first embraced.*

Candle Lighting

Our program included our vows, and a separate page carried the words we each had written to say during our special candle-lighting ceremony:

JUDITH: We are now going to include in our ceremony a cherished spiritual tradition — the lighting of candles. Candle lighting is often a form of communion with one's God or, as I sometimes say, the Great Spirit. This lit candle represents our eternal energies, alight with the promise of new life.

With the lighting of this candle, I ask the Great Spirit to bless our marriage. May our joining as wife and husband, husband and wife, bring us to a further surrender of one unto the other. May our union continue to enlighten our individual paths. May it lighten the heaviness we sometimes feel. And may the products of our individual and coupled energies bring us close to living at one with Thee.

JIM: Candles and their flickering flames possess a very deep and magical meaning. They touch us below our minds and reach images and feelings that are primitive and binding. They provide safety in darkness, and we cling to them. They engender a sense of welcome, and we move toward them. They symbolize awareness. And they stand for life —

both strong and fragile, eternal and momentary, able to spread out to vast distances at great speeds while warming our faces and our noses. But, most of all, for me, it is the power of transformation I see when I watch a candlewick flame with melted wax moving up the wick to be vaporized into heat and light. Through a natural process, one thing becomes something else.

Judith and I have been traveling these past months through a similar natural process, and today we have become transformed. We have accepted and are recognized as husband and wife, wife and husband, an acceptance that is primitive and binding. I light this candle to announce and acknowledge this transformation.

We've included the words of our candle-lighting ceremony because they demonstrate the magic of differences that results when two distinctly different people join their lives together. We had no intention of losing ourselves in a constraining, homogenized union. We made certain to stand apart as individuals while we were joining together as one.

Ahh, Those Cute Children

Children are adorable. They represent innocence and new life. Including flower girls and ring bearers in your ceremony might be the perfect touch. It might even feel timeless, since the use of children in these roles dates back centuries to old Europe. However, we pose the following question: Will children add to the meaning of your wedding ceremony or not? Are they worth the risk that their immature understanding of what's required of them could throw your wedding out of control?

Young children are unpredictable. They have short attention spans. Stay conscious of the risks you take when you include them. If they become frightened by the unusual attention, or seek *more* of the attention by acting up, you two may lose your focus as well as your guests' attention.

Several years ago, when two of our clients, Cassie and Jorian, were married, the groom's three-year-old niece, Ariel, was the flower girl — at the insistence of Jorian's mother. Ariel did her job perfectly, dropping rose petals all along the aisle runner and then taking her position on the mini-stage in the hotel ballroom. However, just as the minister began to direct Cassie and Jorian in their vows, the little girl became restless and grabbed the hem of her dress, lifting it over her head and flashing her lacy pink panties at the crowd. Enjoying the outburst of laughter, she began to lower and raise her dress like a dancer in the Folies Bergère. The more the crowd giggled, the more she performed, spinning around and squealing with delight.

While you might think she was delightful, and no doubt she was, it took two bridesmaids to hold her still and quiet her screams of protest and several more minutes for the crowd to settle down. The couple then continued their vows. But, as Jorian told us later, Ariel had spoiled the tenderness and poignancy of the moment.

Unless you are both exceptionally easygoing and heavily invested in including young children from your families, be aware that they can upstage you at any moment and in many, many ways.

Walking Down the Aisle

Meaningful and creative variations on the theme of dad walking his daughter down the aisle now include mom and dad escorting the bride together, or the bride walking with her mother, with a child or children from a previous marriage, or with her brother(s). And some brides bestow the honor on a beloved grandparent.

The tradition of someone, usually the father, walking the bride down the aisle dates back to times when a groom purchased a bride from her father. As part of the marriage contract, it was the father's duty to literally *give her away* to the groom, because she was now the groom's property.

If you are the bride, you must decide whether you want to be escorted down the aisle and whether you want to be given away. Many girls dream of being given away, and the idea arouses deep feelings. We are not suggesting that you reject the tradition. We just urge you to be aware of the choice you are making.

At the wedding of her college friends, Sydney was impressed as she watched both Drew and LiAnn simultaneously walk down the aisle with their parents. In the program notes they explained that they both wanted to honor the love and support they had received from their parents throughout their lives.

On the other hand, if you are the groom, would you prefer to watch your sweetheart as she makes her way down the aisle by herself, arriving on her own to take your hand? That's the choice Melissa and Dennis made. For her processional she walked unescorted across a bridge that spanned the stream in front of the main house of a beautiful Kentucky horse ranch to meet Dennis, who waited with the minister. Or would the two of you prefer to walk down the aisle together?

Whatever you decide, bear in mind that you are not only

staging your ceremony, but also illustrating the way you want your community to relate to you and the way you relate to yourselves and to each other.

We were married in a Methodist church, where we sang in an informal choir. We chose to have an usher walk Jim's parents, Helen and Ed, down the aisle and seat them in the first row. Then another usher escorted Judith's parents, Helen and Ralph, down the aisle and seated them in the opposite pew. And then, to a beautiful organ and flute duo, we walked down the aisle arm in arm.

After we made our way up the steps to stand at center stage, we took a few moments to welcome our friends and relatives and to thank them for their important roles in our lives. Only then did we begin the ceremony, which included the vows we'd written to each other as our way of marrying ourselves.

The minister had agreed to join us only after we were ready to exchange rings and take the final "I dos." He announced, "I now pronounce you husband and wife," and made everything legal.

Such a processional might not suit your personal style, but we wanted to give you an idea of our choice to literally and figuratively marry ourselves — a choice that continues to be deeply moving and significant to us today.

Backwards, Sideways, or Facing Your Guests

Debbie and Carl met in high school, went their separate ways during college, and reunited when they both joined the Peace Corps. On their wedding day, their guests took their seats, eagerly anticipating a wonderful ceremony and hoping to get a good view.

Entering from a side door, Carl took his place up front and

waited for Debbie to appear. There she was, beautiful and radiant. He mouthed, "I love you" as she made her way down the aisle. Finally she reached him, and they took each other's hands. Then, suddenly, their wonderful faces vanished. Why? Because, following tradition, they turned their backs on their guests.

Rather than taking center stage at their own wedding, they chose to hand it over to the officiant. They could hardly be heard. They certainly couldn't be seen. Who was plainly visible? Someone the majority of guests didn't know and didn't much care about.

Just like Debbie and Carl, the traditional wedding couple has always stood with their backs to the people they've invited. What transpires between the beloved couple is inaudible and invisible. Their subservience to the authority figure to whom they've relinquished their power is made evident by their agreement to allow that person to take the spotlight.

But if Debbie and Carl had at least turned sideways, they would have begun to assert their right to marry on independent terms, and would have been more available to the loving energy from their audience. Facing each other, between the officiant and the guests, would have struck a middle-of-the-road solution to the problem of being seen and heard.

Now, consider the meaning and impact if Debbie and Carl had opted for what we believe to be the most personally powerful and spiritually connected decision: to marry each other while fully facing their guests. The officiant could, perhaps, have stood a stairstep below them or a bit off to the side, as our minister did. This way, the bride and groom would've been visible to everyone and in the direct flow of their community's love and support.

When you face your community, you'll make clear to yourselves — and to all who witness your marriage — not only that you are committing to marry, but that you also intend to take charge of your life together and to rejoice in your freedom to do so.

When the two of you assume control over staging your ceremony, whatever that staging might be, you'll demonstrate your maturity and manifest your willingness to be plainly seen and clearly heard as you speak the vows that make you husband and wife. You will openly proclaim your commitment to each other as your first priority, as well as your determination to be fully visible and present in your marriage. And you'll establish your marriage as one that is to be taken seriously.

You and Your Officiant

For its own reasons, the state requires that you obtain a marriage license. Religious denominations have their own additional requirements. But no matter what these institutions need in order to acknowledge the legality or sanctity of your marriage, remember that no one can ever really marry you — no one except the two of you. Yet a key element of your wedding planning is your selection of officiant.

As we wrote this, Judith's brother, Terry, and his ex-wife, Evey, were remarried at midnight on the bank of the Talkeetna River in Alaska with Denali, the highest peak in North America, behind them. The service was conducted by their grown children, Josh and Erin. There was no minister, no judge. In Alaska, almost anyone can marry anyone.

From Santa Monica, California, Jen, thirty, wrote to *Bride's* magazine, "We are both pediatricians and recently finished up our residencies, so we asked our program director to get a special one-day license to become an ordained minister and marry us. He's such a spiritual mentor that we felt he would be the perfect person to help us begin our life together." As you consider your choice of officiant, you might want to investigate what is possible in your area.

During one of our relationship workshops, a participant, Lydia, complained about a problem she and her groom had had with their minister. "We sat down with the preacher and spelled out what we wanted him to say. And he agreed. But then when we were up there, he went and did what he wanted to do. He added at least ten more minutes to the service and spoiled what we had put together in order to add his two cents."

Meet with your prospective officiant and determine if he or she is open and available to your terms. If not, seriously consider finding someone else.

The Kiss

It's that special moment: your beautiful, wondrous first kiss as a married couple. Will you want to kiss *each other*, or do you prefer that your officiant instruct the groom that he "may now kiss the bride"?

While this might seem to be a small thing, in marriage it's very often the smallest things that grate, that undermine your ability to stay lovingly connected. Don't take any aspect of your staging for granted — and certainly not the kiss.

Unless you believe in specific sex roles, we suggest that you clarify to your officiant that you will kiss *each other*. His or her language will need to support that choice. Also, while it might be embarrassing to kiss in public, this is not the time to relieve your tension by doing something comedic — such as the groom bending the bride into a deep dip and melodramatically kissing her. Nor is this the time to be overly passionate and set off the smoke alarms. Save that for the privacy of your hotel room later that night.

Focus on the spiritual significance of the moment, the joy you wish for your spouse, and the respect you want to feel for all that you do this day. Then you will know the kind of kiss that will be appropriate as well as emotionally moving for the two of you and your guests.

The Recessional

The ceremony is over! You did it. You're officially married. Now you get to make your way back up the aisle.

Many couples simply hold hands, stopping to kiss and hug their parents and other special guests along the way. Others choose a more dramatic or entertaining exit. One bride, Marion, told usabride.com, "Our recessional was a kick. We started out by playing Vivaldi's *Four Seasons* and then cut in with a fast-paced, upbeat song that was special to my husband and me. At that point my husband picked me up and carried me down the aisle and out of the church. Everyone cheered!"

Tracy's three-year-old, Sarah, and four-year old, Kevin, stood between her and her beloved, Mark, as the minister said, "I now pronounce you husband and wife." At that point, Mark, the new stepfather, scooped up his children in either arm, and with tears streaming down his face and Tracy clinging to his arm, the new family joyfully made their way back up the aisle.

While Samantha expected Mendelssohn's "Wedding March," TJ made arrangements with their wedding coordinator to play their song, Shania Twain's "From This Moment On." At first, Samantha was horrified that something had gone wrong. "But then I realized that TJ was singing to me and that he'd set it up. It's my most favorite memory of all."

However you choose to stage your ceremony, stay connected to each other and consciously receive all the positive, loving energy that will be focused on you. Enjoy feeling special, and use that intensity to fuel your determination to live up to the sacred promise you are making.

CHAPTER 12

Beliefs, Luck, and Birdseed

We decided to not see each other before the actual ceremony, to keep things surprising. So, at this cool old ranch in Malibu, there we were in our designated spots before the wedding. I was around a corner. Dean was somewhere else — I wasn't sure where. Then he started pacing, and he paced right over to where I was. He rounded the corner. I looked up. We both screamed. Then we hid from each other, our backs to the wall on either side of the corner. We whispered to each other. "Are you nervous?" "Yeah, you?" "Yeah." It was very sweet and moving.

— Laurel, actress and award-winning filmmaker, California

Historically, many wedding rituals evolved to protect couples against bad luck or to evoke good luck. Bad luck was believed to be caused by jealous curses or evil spirits that were always lurking and ready to attack. The gods were the source of good luck, smiling down on couples and favoring them with fertility and future abundance. No matter how sophisticated we might have become, concern about bad luck and wishes for good luck are still part of our wedding beliefs.

To See Each Other Before — or Not

Easily the most controversial issue associated with old beliefs is the taboo against the bride and groom seeing each other before the ceremony.

We took an informal survey of twenty-one people we know, thirteen women and eight men ranging in age from seventeen to sixty-four. We simply asked, "Why don't the bride and groom see each other before the wedding ceremony?" The answer twenty-one gave, most without thinking, was "Oh, it's bad luck." Once they had blurted out that response, many sheepishly followed by saying something such as "But I don't really believe in bad luck." One woman said, "I know there's no such thing as bad luck, but why take a chance with something as important as your wedding day?"

Some couples, even though they've lived together and shared the same home for years, choose to live apart for several days before their weddings. Even modern, feminist-inclined brides sometimes spend the night before their weddings in a hotel room with their bridesmaids or in their parents' home.

Wedding coordinator Christine Stieber always meets with her couples to explain that this "bad luck" belief stems from the time when marriages were arranged. Quite often, the couple had not yet seen each other at all by the time of the wedding. Since their relationship was not about love but was created for commercial or political gain between families, precautions were necessary to assure that neither one would flee out of fright or repugnance before the knot was tied. As Christine talks with her couples, she jokes with them, asking if either might lose their attraction to the other if they saw each other in the days or hours before their wedding. "They always giggle and laugh at how silly that is."

But What about Your Photographs?

There is a very practical aspect of your decision to see each other or not — the timing of your wedding pictures.

Christine points out, "Right before the ceremony, you will look the very best you'll look all day. The bride's hair and make-up will be freshly done; nobody will have kissed you — leaving lipstick on your cheeks or makeup on the groom's shirt collar — and no one's eyes will be red or puffy from tearful responses to your magic moment. You will also be relaxed and comfortable throughout the photo session before the ceremony, rather than feeling rushed and anxious to get to your guests, who will be impatiently waiting for you at the reception."

Peter Maneen, in Utica, New York, has photographed weddings for over thirty years. He recalls what happened after a wedding that involved two large families and a very large wedding party: "Afterward, it took a long time getting each of the families and all the other different groups together for pictures. The groom could barely conceal his impatience. Then I finally announced, 'Now I'd like to get the bride alone.' To which the groom shouted, 'So would I!'" We admire the groom's good humor, but we're sorry that he had to wait and wait and wait for his darling new wife to join him in their postwedding festivities.

Usabride.com polled its readers for opinions about whether brides and grooms should see each other before their ceremonies. One reader, Cathy, said:

> The best thing about my wedding was that we took the pictures before the wedding. The photographer gave us time alone together in the church. He had placed my husband at the front, near the altar, and told him to keep his back toward the door. Then he brought me into the church and shut all the doors and windows so that it

was only the two of us. I started walking down the aisle toward my husband and called out his name.

The moment he turned around, we both had tears in our eyes. It was just a very special private moment that only the two of us shared. We took some time alone, talking and hugging, before we finally opened the doors to the photographer.

It really, really helped take away the jitters. But it surely didn't take away from the moment I saw him when I started walking down the aisle during the ceremony. It just made everything more special.

On the other hand, Nancy chose to wait:

I almost started to cry when I saw my dear husband waiting for me at the altar, and our best man later told me that he saw my husband's eyes grow very wide with joy when he saw me enter the church. As I stood next to him, he mouthed, "You look beautiful — I love you." I would not have traded that moment for anything! I don't think it would have been as special if we had seen each other for the first time before the ceremony.

That Special Moment — Twice

Wedding photographer Mitzie Pilato, from Norton Hill, New York, takes upward of four hundred shots for each wedding. Meeting with each couple ahead of time, she explains how time-consuming it can be to get all the photos they want.

As with Christine, it's Mitzie's experience that more and more couples now ultimately choose to take their formal photographs before the ceremony. When that is the case, both Mitzie and Christine arrange for the couple to meet in a special room or garden, bringing the groom to where the bride awaits him. Then everyone backs away or goes into another room, leaving them alone for a few minutes.

"Invariably," Christine says, "they take each other's hands, kiss, hug, and then take each other's hands again. They are so thrilled, so happy to be together. And I've had several grooms who thanked me for setting it up so the magical first moment happened twice." As one man said to his fiancée in front of Mitzie, "We always share everything with each other first, and I want to remember, as you're walking down the aisle and everyone is thinking how beautiful you look, that I got to see you first."

There's even the possibility of *three* of these magical moments. A sales associate at a major bridal salon told us, "We love it when the groom helps his fiancée select her gown. It's more exciting, and they have such a good time! It's nonsense that it's bad luck."

Seeing each other beforehand also offers comfort, as Julia Buckham, a Michigan bride, shared. "We opted to have our pictures taken beforehand, which worked out great. We laughed so much and got very silly during the picture-taking. This helped everyone relax and created an atmosphere of joy, joy, joy."

While we received several stories from couples who were glad that they followed convention, their reasons were largely "It's tradition" and "To have that magic moment of seeing each other for the first time." Yet it is clear from our photographers' stories that by taking pictures beforehand, you'll get a double charge of magic! And, of course, you'll save on the stress and worry of running late afterward.

Finally, Christine suggests:

If you're not going to have a coordinator, make sure to appoint one of your friends — who is not in the wedding party — to be your "photographer's assistant." That person's job will be to make sure you get all the photos you want, in the order you want, and to see to it that you both look perfect in every picture. While the photographer can catch most things, you'll want your friend to keep your hair exactly the way it should be, powder your nose from time to time, smooth out your dress and train, straighten your groom's tie or jacket, watch for the angle of your flowers, and fix anything else that would ruin a perfectly wonderful shot — such as lipstick on your teeth. That way, you'll get to relax and know that both your photographer and your friend are watching out for you!

The Beauty of Flowers

No doubt you'll choose to have flowers as part of your ceremony, and no doubt they will be beautiful. But is beauty their only purpose? Or do they possess a deeper significance for you?

The early use of flowers was not merely decorative but was rooted in the ancient belief that nature is alive with evil spirits and that wedding couples — made vulnerable by their time of special happiness — must be protected at every turn. Brides carried bouquets as a barrier, a protective buffer against those demonic forces that would do them harm. At the same time, the use of grains, herbs, and later flowers signified the desire for children.

Roman brides carried herbs under their wedding veils as symbols of fertility and fidelity. During the Elizabethan period, bouquets were certain to include garlic and chives to aromatically ward off unwanted influences. Later, brides began to add fragrant flowers to cover body odors, since bathing was not yet popular and deodorant was nonexistent. And in Victorian times, the groom's boutonniere was usually a flower from the bride's bouquet and was meant as a statement that children were the desired outcome of their ceremony.

Flower girls have been part of weddings for many centuries. The presence of children was a request to the gods to bless the bride with children of her own. The tiny ones sprinkled the road with wheat grains to prevent the bride's feet from touching the ground, where demons were thought to lurk. Later, flowers replaced the wheat, and by medieval times the children had been replaced by a pair of young flower girls dropping rose petals.

Flowers as Symbols

Throughout the centuries, various qualities have been assigned to specific flowers. We selected the following examples from the website of the Society of American Florists (www.aboutflowers.com):

Baby's breath — festivity
Daisy — innocence
Forget-me-not — remember me forever
Gardenia — joy
Orange blossom — desire for fertility
Orchid — delicate beauty
Rose (red) — passionate love
Rose (white) — purity
Sunflower — adoration
Tulip (red) — declaration of love
Tulip (yellow) — hopelessly in love

The Meaning of Your Flowers

Though the meaning of flowers has been interpreted in many ways over the years, the only meaning that is ultimately important is their meaning to you.

What have flowers meant to you throughout your courtship? What flowers might you select based on what you want your flowers and your wedding to signify? How might you incorporate flowers into the ceremony — beyond the bride's bouquet, your wedding party's accessories, and your decorations?

Judith has always loved gardenias, finding their rich, sweet fragrance gloriously elegant — just how she wanted to feel as a bride. And so she carried a bouquet made entirely of gardenias. When you know the meaning certain flowers have for you, you'll enhance their place in your ceremony and celebration.

The Lifting of the Veil

Common to Christian, Jewish, Muslim, and Hindu religious practices, the bridal veil has long stood for purity and chastity. Until the latter part of the twentieth century, the bride's virginity was of supreme importance, as it was supposed to guarantee the lineage of the couple's children. The veil was also thought to protect the bride from ever-present evil spirits and the curses of those who were jealous of her happiness.

It has also been argued that when marriages were arranged and the groom didn't see his bride before their wedding, it was wise to cover her face until after the nuptials were completed, so that he wouldn't run away at the sight of her.

Many brides today prefer a tiara with a veil that falls behind it, clearly revealing their faces from the start. Many others wear a short blusher veil over their faces. Other brides prefer no veil at all. Whatever your choice — and your groom might want to weigh in on this topic — make sure you understand the meaning and motive of your decision.

"It was so moving to have my mother, just before the ceremony, formally send me into my new life. All she did was give me a kiss. Then she got teary-eyed when she placed my veil down over my face," one bride, Veronica, told us. Her face wasn't clearly visible until her groom, Allesandro, lifted the veil to kiss her.

Old, New, Borrowed, and Blue

Many brides still enjoy following the traditional advice that if they wear "something old, something new, something borrowed, something blue, and a silver sixpence in your shoe," good luck will bless their future. While this tradition might not have anything to do with luck, your choices can be memorable and revealing.

Something Old

Incorporating something old acknowledges the continuity of life from the past to the present. Cynthia Brian said, "I wore my mother's wedding gown from 1948 — all satin with a 20-foot train and 102 baby buttons down the back. It was gorgeous. Wearing her gown honored everything she had been and done for me as a mom."

Chris Cahill added, "I wore my mom's wedding dress, which was dearly meaningful to me, and I'm hoping my daughter will follow in the same tradition. My mother's veil had been ruined in storage, so my grandmother made a new one. I worked real flowers into the headband. It was very beautiful."

Something New

With your dreams for the future, your wedding will be a form of initiation. Wearing something new symbolizes your choice to step into that new life and a new identity — as a wife.

Jasmine, a Jungian analyst who specializes in the meaning of symbols, purchased a small rose-quartz heart, a symbol of love, which she tucked in her bra near her heart. Donna wore the pearl earrings Martin had given her for Valentine's Day, little more than a month before their wedding. She wanted to wear something that reminded her of how much fun it was to live with a man who relished gifts and celebrations.

Something Borrowed

Wearing something borrowed will mark your community's participation in the ceremony and their support of your marriage.

Phila Hoopes told us about her choice: "I borrowed my mother's blue garter from her wedding, and I also took my mother's beautiful blue satin negligee from her trousseau on my honeymoon. I'd adored it (and often dressed up in it) when I was a child. Mom loaned it to me as a surprise." Nissa Weaver Van Riper, who described herself as a bit metaphysical, said:

I believe in universal energy (call it God or what you will). I believe that what you put out there is what you will attract. I believe in synchronicities and that you can exert your influence over things more than you think. Wedding traditions (superstitions?) are vestiges of a time when more people believed in magical things. So it was natural for me to follow at least one of them!

At the last minute I discovered I didn't have anything borrowed. My sister, who was my matron of honor, gave me the wedding band she was wearing, which coincidentally had been my maternal grandmother's engagement ring. Grammy had long ago upgraded to the Big Ring at some anniversary or other, so she had had her original engagement ring set with a sapphire and gave me the ring as a gift almost twenty years ago. I actually wore it on my right hand all through high school. When my sister got pregnant and her own band didn't fit anymore, I gave her Grammy's ring, which she wore through all three pregnancies. Her third baby was born only six weeks before my wedding, so she was still wearing the ring on my wedding day and loaned it back to me. Grammy was at the wedding, but I'm not sure she even knows. I'll have to tell her. Anyway, think of all that good karma it had for me on my wedding day!

Something Blue

In the Elizabethan era, both men and women used colored ribbons, called favours, to decorate their wedding costumes. For royalty, the ribbons were predominantly gold or silver. For the rest of the populace, the ribbons were white and blue.

Roni Kaplan wore her sapphire-and-diamond engagement ring as "something blue." Blue was her favorite color, so she also had tiny blue silk flowers woven into the headpiece of her veil as well as the beaded ribbon she wore at her neck. As a singer, she knows that the throat chakra is represented by the color blue. "I feel that expression, the use of my throat to sing and convey what's important to me, is my life purpose. And Adam and I talk about everything. Sometimes we fight, but, hey, that's part of the freedom to be truly loved. So, of course, I wore blue."

Emily Booth Concordia carried her great-grandmother's embroidered hankie as her blue item. She also wore her great-great-aunt's cameo pin as "something old." "It was special for me to have these items with me as I walked down the aisle, because they made me feel as if those people were actually with me on my special day."

And a Silver Sixpence in Your Shoe

Usually a dime in America, a shiny coin in the bride's shoe suggests that no woman should enter marriage without money of her own, and it also symbolizes the couple's future wealth.

Phila said, "I had a sixpence from a trip to Ireland — one of my favorite places. My groom's family emigrated to America from Ireland (they were Quakers on the run with William Penn), and the coin seemed to fit not only the rhyme but that connection."

Should you choose to incorporate these symbols of good luck into your wedding, remember that they are *only* symbols. It is up to you to provide their true meaning, to hold in your hearts and minds the richness of intention that you claim for your life together.

The Wedding Cake

Grains have symbolized fertility throughout many centuries and cultures. In ancient Greece and then in Rome, long before the invention of the wedding cake as we know it today, the groom broke a thin loaf of bread above the head of his bride at the end of the wedding ceremony to help ensure their success in bearing many children. The guests would scramble to grab the crumbs because they were tokens of good luck.

No doubt to help refine the festivities, many miniature loaves were eventually provided and served to the guests. Eventually sesame and honey were added to symbolize the mixed bitter and sweet nature of married life.

Legend has it that in the seventeenth century a French chef thought to put white-sugar frosting on the many little bread-cakes needed for a particular wedding and then stack them together. Voilà! The first wedding cake. After that, the wedding cake became still more refined and elaborate.

Until recent times, the bride had to cut the first slice and eat the first piece of cake so that her fertility would not be "cut into." A single woman desirous of marriage needed only to wrap a small piece of someone else's wedding cake in her left stocking, the same side as the wedding ring, and place it under her pillow. Sleeping with her head on the pillow would bring good luck and dreams of her future husband.

Queen Victoria's cake weighed over 300 pounds, was 9 feet in diameter, and was decorated with marzipan cupids and a statue of Britannia — in ice. Tucked inside the cake were gold charms symbolizing love, for the lucky ones to discover.

Although tradition suggests you save the top layer of your wedding cake in your freezer to eat on your first anniversary, this is often a waste of perfectly wonderful cake. Ours, which we both had loved, was wrapped tightly against freezer burn. Yet on our one-year anniversary, we had no cake to celebrate with because the divine chocolate with buttercream by then tasted like day-old plaster. So, our recommendation: If you want to celebrate your first year with the top tier of your wedding cake, have your baker make a duplicate when the time comes.

Throwing the Garter, the Bouquet, and the Rice

The garter toss dates back to medieval times. Anything that belonged to the bride was thought to bring good luck. If a guest could get hold of one of her gloves or several petals from the flowers she carried, that was a real prize. It was even customary for wedding guests to follow the bride and groom to their marriage bed where, for good luck, they tried to steal off with the bride's garter. To protect his new wife, the groom assumed the responsibility for tossing her garter to the crowd during the reception. The garter toss, now viewed by many as degrading to the bride, is taking its place in the dustbin of wedding lore along with the bride's vow to obey her husband.

The bouquet toss symbolized the bride's generosity as a way she could share her good fortune with the unmarried females at the reception. It was believed that the woman who caught the bouquet would be the next to marry. Many brides today do not throw their bouquets, but give them to a favorite friend or relative as a gift of appreciation having nothing to do with the forecast of marriage.

The practice of throwing rice also symbolizes the wish for good luck and good life. Since grains have a long-standing association with growth and new life, throwing them on the couple once was meant to increase the bride's fertility. Today many couples prefer to have their guests blow bubbles. With bubbles there is no pain on impact, no slippery footing, no need for cleanup, and no potential harm to birds or other animals who could eat the rice. Other couples, who still want to be showered by their guests' blessings, select ecologically preferred birdseed or rose petals.

Carried Over the Threshold

As far back as ancient Rome, people believed that demons haunted doorways where they waited for the unsuspecting, particularly those who were joyous and happy. Certainly the bride and groom fell into that category. So, should the bride stumble as she crossed the threshold of her new home and her new life, it was believed the marriage was doomed to unhappiness. Taking all precautions, the groom defied the demonic forces by carrying her across the threshold. Today, the bride might be carried across the threshold of a hotel room on her wedding night and then again when the couple enters their home for the first time. What was once considered to be an essential protection against bad luck is now simply a fun, romantic gesture.

Now It's Your Turn

While we've not covered all the many beliefs that surround the marriage process, we've given you a flavor of their origins. If your attraction to certain customs sets you on a treasure hunt for new personal meanings and modern interpretations, that's wonderful. After all, what were once superstitions can be reinvented as symbols of personal meaning, blending the old with the new. Then your modern-day wedding will be as colorful and romantic as any that have gone before.

CHAPTER 13

Receiving the Future at Your Reception

My maid of honor gave us the best gift: the gift of time! Every so often she would squeeze my hand or tap me on the shoulder and remind me to look around, to take it all in. Then Brett and I would do the same thing. We'd just stand there holding hands, receiving everyone who was there for us. Because of my maid of honor, we not only have our video and photographs, we have all those precious memories.

— Carolyn Mattrice, stockbroker, Texas

*H*ow can you, as a smart couple, most fully receive the loving wishes of those who will be with you and share your joy at your reception? What your guests will want, more than free food or carefully wrapped favors, is to know that it matters to you that they are with you — in other words, that you're receiving the gift of their presence. When you hold *receiving* as your guiding value, you can design and produce a reception that will make everyone feel involved and cared for — most particularly the two of you. After all, the root of the word *reception* is *receive*.

So often, however, receptions are designed to impress the guests and their true purpose is lost. That's because few couples seriously consider the impact of the reception — the first party they will host as an officially married couple — on themselves and on those they care about most. To avoid this, you can create an after-wedding event of rich substance and meaning — no matter how modest or lavish — that will honor you as you honor those who are there to rejoice with you.

Starting Your Marriage

You're now husband and wife, and it's time to celebrate! What would be most fun for the two of you? Do you value most what your reception will look like and what others will think of it? Or is your goal to be intimate and share yourselves with your family and friends?

If you are more concerned with what others might think, be aware that your attitude places you in a second-rate position in your own minds and in the minds of your guests, whether anyone is conscious of it or not. But if your reception is a time for the two of you to fully share the spotlight and open-heartedly receive the love, support, and enjoyment your guests will offer, you'll establish a pattern of active receiving and overt gratitude that can sustain you throughout your life together.

Timing It Just Right

Whether you plan your reception as a short get-together immediately after your ceremony or as a long weekend party several months after your wedding, make sure you respect your own social comfort and the way you want to interact with your guests.

Since Lindsey and Bennett married while still in graduate school and wanted a no-frills affair, they invited only their close-knit group of friends and immediate family and held their ceremony in the campus chapel. A lovely reception with finger food and cake immediately followed, and the event lasted little more than an hour.

On the other hand, Hannah told us, "I made sure my reception lasted long enough — six hours instead of the usual four or five — so that I had time to eat, talk to everyone, and dance and dance and dance, mostly with my darling Gary. Many of my friends were in tears at the end of the day because they felt like it went by too fast."

Beth and Mark wanted a relaxed and unrushed reception so they could visit with all their guests, some of whom would travel thousands of miles just to be there. So Beth and Mark designed a daylong event at their own home. They both described it as "the most fun we've ever had in a single day."

Dana and Marty had a very private wedding, but they created a memorable three-day weekend four months later for forty close friends and family.

These are just a few examples of the freedom available to you — you can rejoice and celebrate in any way you want. The key to your decision might be summed up by Ron, who told us, "We remember our wedding, the vows, our terrific reception, and our wonderful, loving guests. And, most important, we had a *great time!*"

Your Introduction

If you choose to arrive at your reception after the guests, you might want to be introduced. If so, we recommend that you not share the spotlight with your wedding party. They have already been introduced in your program, and the reception is for you and you alone. You might want your bandleader or DJ to introduce you, and you can use your introduction to establish the mood and tempo of your party. Jennifer reported to usabride.com, "As we were introduced, we were escorted by a troupe of African dancers and drummers who sang and danced in tribute to our new union. The guests [loved] the large and *fabulous* entrance!"

Very Young Guests

If you invite children to your wedding, by all means give them a separate party area so they won't become bored.

Jack invited ten young nieces and nephews along with Sherri Lynn's four. As Jack told us, "We had 210 people at our reception and 42 were kids, who had a much cheaper menu. We set up several game tables, with coloring books, crayons, different kinds of paper, puzzles, games, and lots of stuffed animals. Our neighbor's teenage daughter felt shy about being at the 'grown-up party,' so we gave her ten dollars to oversee the little ones. It was perfect. Everyone had a great time, and the parents didn't have to worry."

Table Markers

Bridal couples differ on whether table markers are helpful. One bride, Noni, wished she hadn't bothered with a seating chart. "Some people sat where I'd put them, but lots of people switched."

On the other hand, if you want a more formal seating arrangement, you still can be as personal and creative with your table markers as with all your wedding's other elements. One couple wrote key words that described what they valued in their relationship — *Intimacy, Play, Freedom, Caring, Spirituality, Thoughtfulness, Generosity,* and *Gratitude* — on large cards placed on wands in the middle of their floral table centerpieces.

One groom, Knut, made cards that marked milestones in his courtship with Alicia: *Knut and Alicia Meet, Our First Date, Our First Kiss, Our First Weekend Away, Knut Meets Alicia's Parents, Alicia Meets Knut's Parents, Knut Pops the Question,* and *Alicia Says YES!*

Designing Your Cake

Your cake can be as symbolic of your relationship as your vows. Meg and Ross both belong to the Sierra Club and love to hike, so they designed their cake as a beautiful mountain, with a little couple in hiking outfits standing on top.

If you have children, take a cue from Lakisha and Greg, who had their bakery make three small round cakes decorated just like their main wedding cake, each with one of their children's names on it. The little cakes were positioned around the large one, and flowers joined them all together. The couple helped each child to cut the little cakes, and then they all took turns feeding one another. Theirs was not just a wedding, but two families publicly joining themselves as one.

Think about cakes *after* the wedding, too. Jeff Buckham surprised his wife, Julia, with a theme cake for a party in the loft of their family barn four months after their ceremony. As Julia described it, "The decorated barn looked like the set of *Oklahoma!* It totally exceeded any expectations I could have imagined. And one of the best parts of the whole day was when my husband surprised me with this incredible cake he'd created with the help of his children, nieces, mom, and sister-in-law. It included a barn with a silo, the sun, sheep, pigs, cows, hay, and a tractor. It was so cool. It was one of the best moments of my life."

Cutting the Cake

When you cut your cake and take turns feeding a bite to each other, you will symbolically pledge to nourish and care for each other and to share in the goodness of life from that day on.

While we have faith that, as a smart couple, you would never consider indulging in the current craze of smashing cake in each other's faces — we have heard far too many stories of husbands or wives surprising their mates with a face full of frosting. We've even heard of the bridal couple turning on their maid of honor and best man with pieces of cake that appeared to be aimed for each other. This is not funny. It is abuse — and it is publicly condoned abuse at that, when guests laugh and applaud.

Remember, how you treat each other and those around you during these first hours of your marriage signals how you want to be treated throughout your marriage.

Dancing Becomes You

Of course you will have your first dance together. It's traditional, and a wonderful ritual. Have you thought about it? Do you know what it means to you? What about the dancing that will follow?

As Carrie Lynn told usabride.com, "The best thing about our wedding was that we had a friend (also an usher) sing our wedding-dance song and had all of our guests surround us as we danced. It was so beautiful, and it made everyone feel like they were a part of us! When we all watched the video the next day, there wasn't a dry eye in the room!"

Yijie and Hong Mei met at the Los Angeles Jewelry Mart, where he managed a pearl company and hired Hong Mei as marketing director. They enlivened their reception with periodic "pearly moments." Each time their DJ rang a bell, he pulled a guest's name, and that guest got to choose a pearl from a display case. To make it even more fun, that person had to give the pearl to whomever he or she chose to dance with.

Tina told us that since "a lot of our friends are gay, we had men dancing with men at the reception, and my husband, Richard, a ballroom dance teacher, danced with several men, switching off leading and following. These are all dance teachers and expert dancers, so the crowd loved watching this expression of love-filled freedom and talent."

When Dixie, a former client of ours, was about eight years old, her parents recorded her singing "I'm Dreaming of a White Christmas." She told us how special it was when, at her December wedding, her mom had the DJ play the recording during Dixie and her dad's first dance. Everybody teared up, especially the bride and her father.

Lee and Brittany received a standing ovation after their first dance. Living in Miami, they admired the Cuban salsa. But only in preparation for their reception did they master the moves. In their program they credited Carlos Acevedo (www.salsa-rhythms.com) with teaching them to go all out on the dance floor.

Joellen made sure to dance with her mom, not just her dad. "Since we had a rock-and-roll blues band and both of my parents are good dancers, we also rocked out as a threesome."

And as Celeste said: "I wish I had danced more with my husband. Besides being fun, it was the only way we had some alone time with each other."

Touching Toasts

Encourage those who will make toasts to speak from their hearts and to be as personal as possible. Unless you enjoy jokes, make sure they know you don't want any — of any kind.

Many people are uncomfortable speaking in public, so they might be tempted to give a generic toast, maybe even something they've found in a book, rather than speaking about their relationship with the two of you. That might bore your guests, and make it difficult for you to feel touched or able to receive in any heartfelt way. Remember, it's your reception, so it's perfectly permissible to ask for the types of toasts you'll remember and appreciate.

Jackie said the best gift she received was the toast her maid of honor, Kendra, gave. "We've known each other since kindergarten, and when Kendra started to choke up, having to start and stop again while telling everyone how happy she was for me and for us, I tell you, even the groomsmen, all former football players, were wiping away the tears. What a gift to be so loved by someone who's known me through everything."

Erin Saxton, our producer/PR friend, shared this special moment with us as an example of how off-the-cuff humor can be enormously affectionate:

> Joe, our best man, delivered a speech that had him tearing up. He said that he knew Anders and I got along well because, during our first weekend away together, it rained the whole time, yet Anders came home saying it was the best trip, because we stayed in bed all weekend eating pizza and watching football. He didn't mean to, but Joe implied other episodes as well. This statement went out to an audience of 220 people. The crowd broke out in such a racy laugh that it prompted my dad to say

to my priest, "Father, I'm shocked at this. I had no idea Erin liked *pizza!*" Everyone roared, understanding the depth of my dad's love for Anders and me in just that one statement.

Favors

For centuries, dating back to the Greeks, couples' traditional thank-yous to their guests have been *bonbonnières*, five sugared almonds enclosed in tulle or lace. But are thank-yous in the form of little gifts really enough to express your gratitude? And consider the time and expense, the hassle and disappointment if you find your favors left behind, which we know happens over and over.

No one attends a wedding concerned about whether they'll get a favor. But they do want to know you care that they are there. So, at some point, stand, take the microphone if necessary, and tell your guests what it means to have them there with you, that you're grateful to receive their congratulations and to feel their support. The best favor you can give your friends and family is to let them know how much they've touched you just by being there.

If you still want to provide some form of favor, consider charity favors. That way, everyone will know that your money went to a good cause. You could make up a card for each guest telling them that a donation was made in his or her name to a charity of your choice. We know a couple who chose to plant trees in the name of each guest who attended their October wedding. They made arrangements through the National Arbor Day Foundation (www.arborday.org/join/tictim/index.cfm), which plants trees in national forests that have been damaged by fire, insects, or disease. They created cards that included a picture of a tree and a description of the donation, plus this statement: "Joining together in the forest of the world, we are all one. This gift was made in your name to help our planet thrive."

Receiving Gifts

It goes without saying that you won't invite people in order to get gifts — or to pay for your catering bill. Yet, among younger brides, a kind of underground "rule" has recently emerged stating that guests should pay as much for their gifts as their meals will cost the hosts.

Guests are never required to give you a gift. Never. Should you be disappointed in a gift, then perhaps your guest is giving you more honest information about his or her character than you'd previously understood, or the gift reflects their limited feelings for you or simply their limited finances. Or perhaps you are being stretched spiritually, being encouraged to remember the spirit of love with which the gift was given and to recognize that the gift itself might simply not be to your taste.

In any case, the ability to receive gifts without cynicism or criticism is a spiritual discipline and a gift to yourselves. Open your heart and embrace reality as it is — that is the mature grace of conscious receiving.

Memorable Moments

Obviously, we can't cover every possible option you can consider when you're designing your postwedding party to be personal, inclusive of your guests, and reflective of all that is truly meaningful to you. But we do want to share a moment that Melanie Hodge and Brian Garcia planned for their wedding.

Melanie's great-grandfather on her father's side collected butterflies and moths, and his extensive collection now resides in the Museum of Natural History on the campus of the University of Southern California. As Melanie told us, "In honor of her husband's passion, my great-grandmother Oma — she was born in Holland — wore only clothing that had butterflies on it. She was very loving, and we all feel very connected to her spirit. When we see a butterfly, we always say, 'There's Oma; she's with us.'" So Melanie and Brian wanted to honor Oma by releasing butterflies during their outdoor party.

A Tender Time

The stereotype of weddings allows for only grace and joy. But what of other feelings that could surface at your after-wedding party?

After all, less rosy feelings certainly can arise at such a momentous time. As Art Klein shared with us, "Our dinner and reception were kind of tense. There were many family rivalries, lots of behind-the-scenes stuff, going on. In the midst of that, we had just publicly made a clear acknowledgment of our love, something that was terribly fragile and was now up for everyone else to bandy about. We felt we had to be living symbols of love, of its myriad and miraculous possibilities, and we felt pressure not to fail at love."

So do not be surprised if unusual feelings emerge at your reception. You are human and need to take good care of yourselves. For example, if you are concerned that someone might behave badly or act rudely and/or possessively toward you, consider these possibilities:

❖ *Ahead of time, ask your attendants and ushers to keep an eye out for troublemakers or those who might impose upon* the two of you. Ask them to help you by stepping in to redirect these people away from you and/or to ask them to step outside so they will no longer disrupt the festivities.

❖ Do not make excuses for your guests' bad behavior. It is not your job to play cop, therapist, or a priest hearing confession. Do not hesitate to tell people that you'd be glad to deal with their issues at another time (if that's true) but that you are not available now. Or you might need to simply say, "Your problems with so-and-so or such-and-such are none of my business. Please don't talk to me about this."

❖ Should any family friction erupt, do not hesitate to step in and ask that the conversation continue outside so it will not interfere with your celebration. If they refuse, ask a couple of your ushers to invite those people to leave.

❖ Most important, stay connected to each other. If the two of you need to step into a hallway or the parking lot to blow off steam or figure out how to handle a problem guest or regain your bearings, make sure you remain fully supportive of each other. Return to your reception with a plan in mind, holding hands and unwilling to compromise your desire for a loving, joyous day.

It's All for You

You face a lot of organizing when planning a reception, even if you work with a wedding coordinator (which we recommend if you'll hold a large event). So, remember these key points:

❖ Plan well, then put someone in charge of overseeing your reception. Don't fuss with the details on your wedding day. Trust that love and joy will take care of what's important.

❖ *Make sure to eat before your ceremony and at the reception. So many brides talk about missing out on the food and feeling faint because they didn't eat beforehand. And if you love your cake, eat lots of it!*

❖ *Enjoy, to the best of your ability, being the center of attention. Don't hide out at the bar or go off with your friends. Smart couples are mature enough to stay present with their guests.*

❖ *Ask someone to occasionally tap you on the shoulder during the reception to remind you to look around so you can be conscious of all that is happening in your honor.*

❖ *Make sure you stay connected with each other, and dance together as much as you want. It is not your job to entertain guests who look lonely.*

❖ *Don't let the photographer, caterer, or DJ control your event. Stay in charge, or appoint someone to do it.*

❖ *Don't drink too much. Why risk a hangover or passing out? (Perhaps more to the point, if you'll need to become unconscious on your wedding day, why are you getting married at all?)*

❖ *Remember why you created the event — to receive the love and support of all those near and dear to you. So, receive, receive, receive!*

CHAPTER 14

Celebrations Galore

*Since we'd purchased a fixer-upper several months before our small,
intimate wedding, we decided to hold an open-house weekend for our
reception. That way, we didn't need to worry about people's schedules
and we got to spend more time with our guests. We also enjoyed showing off our rags-to-riches renovation.*

— Jerome, plumber and electrician, Nevada

*I*f the traditional one-day wedding, in which the reception
immediately follows the ceremony, doesn't fit your needs or
desires, or if you want to add unusual personal elements to your
reception, remember that there is no set pattern you must follow. In fact, we were so impressed with the vast array of creative,
unique, and deeply love-filled before- and after-wedding events
we heard about from friends, survey respondents, former clients,
wedding vendors, and others that we decided to devote this
chapter to some of their stories to help you to further open your
imagination.

The Night Before

Nicole Avril and Todd Lapin dubbed their nonrehearsal dinner for 350 friends and family members "The Night Before." Customizing their nuptial weekend to fit their late-thirties maturity and San Francisco's Mission District lifestyle, they held the Night Before party in a parking lot adjacent to a warehouse. There they set up a bar and a makeshift bandstand where musician friends took turns playing, and all their closest friends pitched in to help. Todd contracted to have a huge taco truck supply all-you-can-eat Mexican food (which cost them less than a thousand dollars).

As Todd told *ReadyMade* magazine, which covered their event, "I wanted my family [from New Jersey, and the Avrils from Long Island] to see the creative energy and support Nicole and I received from those we've gathered around us." Rather than the typical ceremony — "Dinner, dance, cake, dance, go home — it's so predictable" — Todd and Nicole wanted to create the "down-home feel of a Mexican *zócalo*, or village square." And succeed they did. Everyone mingled over tacos, listened to music, and prepared for the new marriage they would witness the next day.

A Valentine's Day Surprise

Diana MacGregor had been married before and would have preferred a private ceremony. But her fiancé, Chris, wanted to do something that would include his parents and his nine-year-old son, since Chris had never been married. As Diana tells it:

> We invited everyone (our immediate family and three very close friends, twenty-five people total) to a Valentine's

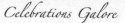

Day luncheon at Schuler's Restaurant in Marshall, Michigan. We both have sons who are nine, and they sat at the head table with us. Schuler's made the cake, and we had red roses in rose bowls for Valentine's Day centerpieces.

Then, with everyone there, the mayor of Marshall, John Miller (who we'd never met — it was all arranged by phone), walked in and performed a very personal, intimate little wedding (just like he'd known us forever!). And there we all were, ready for our celebration luncheon. It was a most memorable day, just enjoying our wedding with our closest friends and family.

More Vows of Love

We learned about Katey Brunini, fine jewelry business owner, and Johnny Marotta, builder, from *Bridal Guide* magazine (July/August 2002). Katey discovered she had traveled the world only to find true love in her next-door neighbor in San Diego, on the other side of the white picket fence that separated their driveways.

They exchanged their vows after a four-day fiesta in Cabo San Lucas, Mexico, where they enjoyed time with their friends, played in the surf, and watched while their sixty-five guests developed new friendships. On the final day they exchanged vows at sunset on a private deck. Then, for the reception, the bride and groom led the guests — and a mariachi band — down a petal-strewn path to a villa owned by friends.

The most precious moment for Katey came when Johnny's children, Corey, 23, and Nicole, 25, toasted the bride, their new stepmother. As Katey told Lisa Marie Rovito of *Bridal Guide*, "Corey and Nicole told the story of a big rock in the Colorado River that they love to jump off of. They'd been going there with their dad for years, and no woman Johnny had ever brought would jump, except me. They made me cry when they said they'd finally found the person who would jump with them."

For Katey and Johnny there were layers and layers of love vows that permeated and punctuated their special celebration.

Gathered Together — But Not at the Wedding

Dana and Marty Ostermiller produced and paid for both a private wedding and a wedding celebration weekend that took place four months later. Driven by Dana's sudden realization that she wanted her married name on her diploma when she graduated from medical school, and that the school required a minimum two days' notice to process the change, Dana and Marty rushed to the courthouse in Albany, New York, to get their marriage license. But they had to wait twenty-four hours before marrying according to state law.

So they called the Lake Placid Lodge in the Adirondacks and booked a spectacular cabin. Upon their arrival they were surprised to learn that the dining room was closed. But, because the lodge knew the reason for their visit, a waiter was sent to serve them a candlelit dinner in their cabin. Dana told us:

> The next morning I wore my favorite twenty-nine-dollar sundress from Express and Marty wore khakis, a freshly ironed shirt, and flip-flops. Four of us gathered on the dock overlooking the lake: Marty, myself, the justice of the peace (whom we'd found the day before), and the hotel receptionist, who doubled as our witness and photographer. The justice of the peace conducted a simple, outstanding ceremony with traditional vows, readings from the spiritual poet Rumi, and a Native American prayer.

Afterward, the hotel staff spoiled us with a champagne breakfast, and together we made our own private toasts. It was raining by then, so we went back to our cabin, lit a fire and candles, and spent the rest of the day in bed. It was a wonderful, romantic time. Late that afternoon we drove to Lake George, where my family gathered to celebrate both our wedding and my medical school graduation, which occurred the following day.

Four months later, with the ten thousand dollars we would have spent on a traditional wedding, we arranged for forty of our closest friends to join us for what we called our "Montana Fiesta." Our guests paid their way from around the country and then enjoyed an expense-free three-day weekend of adventure, celebration, and time outdoors.

Our invitation was a CD of our favorite music. We expressed the spirit of the weekend on the inside of the jacket cover and supplied a list of what to pack, including hiking and riding boots, sleeping bags, and one dressy outfit. The weekend unfolded as a complete surprise for our guests — hiking, picnics, dancing, hot springs, live music, horseback riding, and the last day at a beautiful guest ranch called Mountain Sky. On the final night, with everyone wearing their sexy best, we met on the deck of our lodge for champagne, followed by a long dinner, countless toasts, tears, and lots of laughter.

During the dinner Dana and Marty spoke to the group, saying, "We want you to know how important it is to have you witness our union. We know that it won't always be as easy as the past few days. So we're asking for your help, because we know we will falter. We will need to call on you to help us stay true to the ideals of our marriage that seem so clear right now."

Dana told us, "We have done that. We've called our friends when we needed reminders, when we needed help."

There were still more blessings for Dana and Marty. As a reminder of the weekend, one friend had everyone sign a large parchment with the couple's names at the top. Later it was framed and delivered to them. Beautiful hand-painted flowers adorned either side, and in calligraphy were the words "We, having gathered on September 7–10, 2001, to celebrate the marriage of Dana Cathleen Cronin and Marty Richards Ostermiller, affix our signatures below to bestow our affections and blessings on their union." Marty's sister videotaped the weekend, editing it into a gift she gave them that Christmas. Another friend took still photos and created a beautiful handmade photo album for them.

Dana said, "So many wrote to thank us for how extraordinarily meaningful the weekend was. Many became friends with people who previously were strangers. And Marty was right when he thought that the two singles would hit it off, because they're now engaged to be married. Our experience motivated so many other couples to break free and do what would be particularly meaningful to them."

Home from the Destination Wedding — A Weekend for Three Hundred

Destination weddings have become increasingly popular for many reasons — the location holds special meaning for the couple; the site might arrange everything for a nominal fee; and because there are far fewer guests than at most weddings, the

couple can splurge on extravagances as well as spend quality time with those guests who attend. Consequently, the couple or their parents often hold a large party several weeks or months later, in their hometown or elsewhere. Since the wedding itself is over, the couple can focus on creating a wonderful party, or even a long weekend of close connection and celebration.

Sondra and Aaron, who married amid the ruins of Machu Picchu in May, enjoyed two postwedding parties. The first occurred immediately after their ceremony. Their wedding party/hiking group of eleven headed for Aquas Calientes, where their trekking company had set up a postwedding feast in a local café. Their tour guide had made sure that a local band played traditional Andean music, and Aaron had even been able to arrange for a wedding cake to top off the celebration.

Back home, the couple organized and planned a weekend celebration for three hundred people who made their way to Snoqualmie Pass outside Seattle, Washington. Although their parents helped with the cost, the bride and groom planned the event.

Their official party started on Saturday at 4 P.M., according to Aaron, "and lasted until 3 A.M. Everyone slept over and, after a huge breakfast the next day, they hiked and spent time together before they departed for home." Sondra added, "We took the friends and family who would have made up our wedding party out the day before, including a boat cruise of Lake Washington and Lake Union and then a salmon dinner at our favorite restaurant."

Aaron's advice for other couples: "Make sure you do what makes you happy. Make sure your family and friends aren't left out. But do what you want to do." If you would like to learn more about Sondra and Aaron's experience, visit their website at weddingchannel.com (http://sondraandaaron.weddings.com).

Cross-cultural Wonder

Sarah Rubin and Giuseppe Mavvorotti enjoyed the magic of their differences. Sarah is Jewish and Giuseppe, Italian. The couple met in law school, and she aimed to be a defense attorney, while he hankered for prosecution. And they are now living their dreams. But for their dream wedding they wanted to create a harmonic symphony from their differences.

Married by a modern-thinking rabbi and priest under a brightly colored chuppah, they followed the Jewish tradition of breaking the glass, doing it together and explaining that it was time to celebrate. The crowd enthusiastically called out, "Mazel tov!"

At the reception, guests were greeted by an Italian trio playing mandolins and were served Italian wines. Bride and groom made sure the prime rib and salmon buffet table featured dishes native to both cultures, including antipasto, several pastas, and gourmet make-your-own pizzas, along with borscht, gefilte fish, and potato latkes.

Finally, before dinner, Sarah and Giuseppe gave a special prayer, followed by a performance by a professional soprano who sang "O Mio Bambino Caro," an aria from Puccini's opera *Gianni Schicchi*, with grace and passion. Guests, Italian and Jewish alike, spontaneously held hands, letting tears of love run down their cheeks — and then the party began.

An Aspen Dream Come True

Paige and JC Keeler were married in February on the deck of the Elk Mountain Lodge in Aspen, Colorado, overlooking the mountain range and the valley below. Their ceremony lasted less than an hour and was scheduled at the time when the sun would best warm the deck.

Theirs was no average wedding. As Paige said, "We were deeply blessed that my father wanted to give me my dream wedding, and he could afford what we wanted." Nevertheless, during the year that Paige and JC had spent planning their three-day event, they never took their focus off ensuring their guests would feel cared for, and they never took for granted all the blessings of their unique relationship.

Paige's parents would have preferred a guest list of five hundred, but Paige and JC were clear that they wanted only those people who they loved and who loved them in return. The result was a group of 180, who all flew into Aspen.

Because Paige and JC romantically connected while he was the legal consultant for her art gallery in Manhattan, Mixed Greens (www.mixedgreens.com), theirs was a wedding of beauty and artistic creativity in every way possible. For instance, as Paige explained, "Everyone's place card for the reception was framed in a sterling-silver snowflake keepsake from Tiffany's."

The wedding couple didn't want to just shower their guests with things. As Paige told us:

> We also showered them with love, for we made sure to include every person who came to the wedding in every single event. There were no "family and wedding party only" events. Everyone there was considered family.
>
> The wedding took place in a circle. We were in the middle, surrounded by friends and family on all sides — reiterating how important each and every person was to us. We wrote and memorized our own vows and didn't share the vows with each other before the wedding. The ceremony included our minister asking everyone witnessing our union to promise to love and support us through good times and bad. They responded with a resounding "We will!"

It was so important not to lose connection with each other that we made a pact to look around every half hour or so to make eye contact or join each other. That was our way of protecting ourselves against becoming overly invested in socializing with our guests at the expense of our own connection.

To make sure everyone (including us) enjoyed the reception, we offered them a private concert by one of JC's and my favorites — Lyle Lovett. We had fears of his overshadowing the wedding, but he was perfect. Everyone thoroughly enjoyed the surprise — we didn't tell a soul, not even immediate family, that he would be there. Lyle was our gift to our guests, not to mention a gift to us as well! Our first dance was to "She's No Lady, She's My Wife," which was perfect for the very informal attitude we had fostered throughout the weekend. Lyle even signed CDs for us to place in everyone's "Morning After" goodie bags.

Another of the "gifts" we gave our guests was JC's and my full attention. We worked with an unbelievable wedding planner who took care of all the details so that we could spend every possible moment with our guests. We were not harried or worried at any time and could relax and enjoy as much of the event as our guests were enjoying. And because the wedding lasted three days, we got quality time with everyone.

After Their Second Wedding

Terry and Evey married for the second time, as we explained in chapter 11, by the river in the small town of Talkeetna, Alaska. When their short evening ceremony was over, they and their two grown children, who had officiated, and two witnesses walked across the bridge over the Talkeetna River and back into town for a party in the beer garden of the historic Fairview Inn.

Although Terry and Evey were in Talkeetna only for the summer, they were so embraced by the community that, with no formal invitations, over two hundred people joined in their "super-high-energy" party, which lasted until 4 A.M. Terry and Josh, their son, played music, and plenty of other musicians brought their instruments to the informal jam session. However, the most touching moment was when Terry sang in Spanish to his former and new bride the Los Lobos classic "Volver, Volver" (To Return, To Return) *"a tus brazos otra vez"* — "to your arms once again."

Terry said it was "the most fun and touching party" he'd attended in his life. "It occurred because we got involved in the community and made wonderful connections, and everyone wanted to celebrate our special second-time-around brand-new marriage."

Two Parties for One Wedding

Mike and Judy Collier Lynne had known each other earlier in their lives, but had married and divorced other people before realizing they belonged together. In chapter 10, you read about Judy's grown daughters, Kim and Trisha, who escorted Judy and Mike and joined them together during their wedding ceremony.

But that is only part of their story. They knew that after the wedding they would want to celebrate. But how? Judy wanted an elegant dinner for sixty following their ceremony beside a beautiful lily pond shimmering with gold and white koi at a Santa Barbara hotel. She envisioned a relaxing candlelit evening where everyone would be seated in a beautiful garden room with a view of the ocean. Mike, who had served in Vietnam, wanted a party for 130 that he could ride into on his motorcycle, wearing a T-shirt and black leather jacket.

Clearly they had a problem. Wedding coordinator Christine Stieber came to the rescue. "Have two parties," she suggested. "You can afford it, and you'll both be happier that way."

So right after their wedding Judy and Mike hosted a gourmet dinner where they cut their three-tiered wedding cake topped with crystal swans and fresh yellow roses, danced to romantic music, and enjoyed a relaxed, intimate evening with sixty of their closest family and friends. Christine honored Judy's love of the koi pond by creating fishbowl centerpieces, Each held two live goldfish and floating flowers. One guest at each table received a tiny goldfish sticker on his or her place card, which meant they got to take the bowl (protected with a plastic food container and mini–shower cap) home in a box, complete with fish food and a tiny net.

Judy and Mike spoke to the group, acknowledging the loving support they had received from their guests and thanking them for all they had contributed to their relationship and their wedding. They also gave a special tribute to Judy's parents, who would soon celebrate their sixtieth wedding anniversary.

Then, two weeks later, in a junior high school multipurpose room, Christine helped Judy and Mike decorate for a fifties-style sock hop complete with a black-and-white checkerboard dance floor. And Mike did indeed ride in on his motorcycle, wearing his T-shirt and black leather jacket.

And then the fun began. Guests were greeted by a sign that read "Welcome to the Gym" and featured photos of Judy as a student nurse and Mike in his Green Beret uniform — just the way they had looked when they first met. The women arrived in ponytails, poodle skirts, and pedal pushers, while the men stuck to jeans, white T-shirts with rolled-up sleeves, black leather jackets, and ducktails. Polaroid cameras were available for the 130 guests to capture one another for the guest book, where they wrote their messages to Judy and Mike under their photos — just as in a high school yearbook. The DJ played all the best from the fifties and sixties while dance instructors helped guests remember how to Twist, Stroll, and do the Hand Jive. There were bubble gum–blowing contests, hula hoop contests, Coke-glass centerpieces, and bridesmaids dressed as Pink Ladies from the movie *Grease*, wearing pink jackets Christine had rented from a theater company.

The printed menu for "Mike and Judy's Diner" featured hamburgers, cheeseburgers, hot dogs, chili dogs, fries, onion rings, milk shakes, and floats. There was no wedding cake this time, just Mike's favorite: brownies. When the time arrived, there was Mike with his Green Beret jungle knife and his ladylove Judy to help him cut into the enormous sheet of brownies. Behind the scenes, to avoid a time crunch, Christine had arranged 130 precut brownie squares with a candle in each. After the Pink Ladies had served every guest and Christine's assistants had lit the candles, Christine invited everyone to make a wish for themselves and, as they blew out their candles, to make a wish for Mike and Judy. The evening ended as the photographer took a group picture of all the guests surrounding Judy and Mike on the motorcycle and beaming at the newlyweds with love and affection.

While we heard this story from Christine, Judy added her own thoughts: "Mike and I were so grateful that we were able to find this special way to celebrate our differences and to show how love and caring are about sharing and honoring each other's unique preferences. We believe that the best relationships are those to which each partner contributes something unique that brings added dimension and new adventure to their life together."

Receiving with Love

Our friend Magdalena Golczewski, former violinist with the Metropolitan Opera Orchestra, now plays occasionally for large upscale weddings. She recalls how one couple, Ashley and David, who married on the lawn at the Catskill Mountain House, one of the oldest hotels in upstate New York, acknowledged their guests and made them all feel special.

"It was so touching when they took the stage at their reception to say, 'Without you, none of this would have happened. We not only married each other; we have acquired a family, which is you.' With their arms wide open, they looked at their guests, beaming at their new family, embracing them, thanking them, and receiving them. Everyone was so touched, and it expressed the best of what weddings are all about."

CHAPTER 15

The Real Romance of Your Honeymoon

Some of the sweetest intimacy and romance we experienced on our honeymoon occurred while we were in the hot tub overlooking the Acapulco coastline. I told Dan I was sad that the wedding was over. He told me he was relieved that it was over. We knew we could be headed toward a big fight, but instead we talked about it, really talked about it, and ended up feeling a new understanding and compassion for each other. That led to a wonderful afternoon making love.

— Courtney, hairstylist, North Carolina

It's easy to imagine that your honeymoon will be relaxing, adventure-filled, and divinely sexual. For some couples, that's actually the case. But, so often — especially if you leave right after your reception — you can look forward to unexpected conflicts and delightfully odd surprises. Because no matter how long you've been together and no matter how much you've traveled together, now you are husband and wife, wife and husband. Permanently. Committed forever. It's a brand-new world.

The Honey of the Moon

In ancient times, when brides were captured, the groom had to keep his "bride" hidden away from her people, because they would come searching for her. So the couple hid out for a full moon cycle, or one month. If the bride stayed with the groom for that length of time, it was understood that she was his for life. Fortifying her with mead made of fermented honey, the groom attempted to keep her submissive so that she would eventually surrender to their new relationship. With the magic combination of the moon cycle and honeyed mead, we now have the "honeymoon."

Losing Your Virginity — of a Sort

Although the bride is no longer captured by her husband, she can still become captured and enraptured by the dream of being a princess at her wedding. Then, when the last dance is over and the champagne gone, it's time for the first stage of the honeymoon, the wedding night.

These days, society no longer demands physical virginity on the wedding night. Yet the end of the bride's dream day — the finality of having to remove her wedding gown — is often too poignant to endure. A friend confided that immediately after her wedding, her work schedule brought her home earlier than her husband. So, each day for a month, she put on her wedding gown and wandered around the house, looking at herself in the mirror, remembering the wedding and wishing it weren't over. Another woman told us about her friend's experience in dealing with the finality of it all:

> In the hotel room with her husband, when it was time to take off her wedding dress, she cried like a baby. For

hours, she sat on the bed in her elaborate gown and veil crying and crying because she knew that if she took her dress off she would never put it back on. She couldn't deal with that, so she sat there fully clothed, refusing to budge. Her husband, after hours of coaxing, finally got her to take it off. But he swore that at one point he thought that she'd end up delivering their first child in that dress!

Many women begin dreaming in childhood of the day when they will be the wedding princess, more beautiful than ever before. However, all too soon their glass slippers turn into terry cloth or even plastic. Yet they have had no preparation for the postwedding blues, the letdown when their time as princess-for-a-day comes to an end and regular life breaks the spell.

For their first night as husband and wife, Mitzie and Shane Pilato wisely chose to return to the apartment where they lived together. It offered much-needed comfort and safety in which to make the transition. When the time came for Mitzie to take off her gown, Shane first photographed her in it. Then Mitzie displayed it gracefully over a chair. "We got our guest book, our toasting glasses, my bouquet, and the gifts and took more pictures of each other sitting on the couch, toasting each other, and opening our presents. And we both got teary. It allowed us to continue celebrating and make a gradual shift back into our regular life."

Take Your Time Leaving

Mitzie's one regret is that they left for their honeymoon the next day, leaving fifteen out-of-town relatives behind. Mitzie, herself a bridal photographer, was born in Costa Rica. Her relatives, with whom she'd grown up, had traveled all the way to New

York for her wedding. "Shane and I went to the Poconos in Pennsylvania. But rather than having a great time, I missed being with my out-of-town family so much that we cut our trip, a five-day package, by two days and came home. I tell all the brides that I photograph, 'Don't leave right away for your honeymoon. The process of planning and preparing for your wedding is involved, so take some time afterward to relax with friends and relatives.'"

Even though Monica and Forrest had a small wedding, they nevertheless waited a day to leave for the shore, where they'd rented a condo. "We spent Sunday with our family and opened our gifts," Forrest said. "It was very relaxing and a nice way to end the wedding weekend."

Melanie and Brian left for their honeymoon six months after their wedding. They stayed to the end of their reception and spent as much time as possible with their out-of-town guests. Melanie was very clear about their decision: "Planning the wedding is such an important time, such an amazing process. We wanted to focus only on that."

Brian explained, "We went where we could do so many things — rafting, hiking, diving. It was endless. And it wasn't very expensive, so we could stay for two weeks. Plus, we didn't need to plan our trip until after the wedding."

Melanie added, "Most important, that way it gave us something else to look forward to — instead of the letdown after it was all over."

Taking a Mini-Honeymoon

You might not want to go away right after your wedding, or perhaps you can't afford to travel yet or family demands make it impossible. But there's no need to act as if it's business as usual.

On the weekend after your wedding, take a two-day mini-honeymoon. Include anything and everything that would be fun and intimate, such as taking a candlelit bubble bath together or going to a part of your town or a nearby town you've never been to where you can poke around, shop for bargains, and eat in a local dive. And, of course, don't forget those imaginative romantic sexual interludes!

Treat your first married weekend as a glorious, joyous vacation. Perhaps this is a time to create an altar together, if that fits your spiritual beliefs. Or plant a garden that will grow with your marriage. Or make your favorite, maybe even forbidden, foods. Indulge your passions; rejoice in being together. But the cardinal rule is — only you two — no one else. You'll do plenty of socializing in the years to come.

Not What You Expected

No matter how well you've planned for your honeymoon, you have no control over the weather, flight schedules, overbooked hotels, and the like. Keep yourselves open to the unexpected, which will, no doubt, occur.

During our honeymoon, in the south of France, if it had not been for a car-rental office that was unexpectedly closed at noon on a Monday (the clerk had left for lunch) we would have missed hearing a magnificent choir in a medieval cathedral that Jim had discovered when he traveled through Europe twenty years earlier.

Our friends Art and Pat were married in New York City. Their honeymoon, as Art tells it, was nothing like they had expected, and yet was even more remarkably romantic because of it:

We decided to drive upstate and stay at our new mountain home. On the way up it started to rain and sleet. At a rest stop at the foot of the mountains, I declared that it was unsafe to go on and likely to be snowing on the mountaintop. Pat said that was crazy; we should get to our nice new home. So I, feeling like I would be a chicken if I didn't keep driving, relented.

We didn't get to our new home for two days. By the time we were twenty minutes from our destination, fourteen inches of snow had fallen, and all major roads were closed. It would reach twenty-eight inches by morning. We stayed at a small resort that was closed but took pity on us. The only food available was locked behind the glass of a vending machine that wasn't working. I wrestled with that machine until something clicked and it surrendered its chocolate treasures — which served as dinner that evening and breakfast the next morning.

After we settled in, surrendering to the reality of being there, we soon realized how beautiful it was to be with each other with no distractions. We were safe and warm, protected from the quiet, white, drifting world outside. And, most important, we had each other, which is the finest blessing we've known in this life. Our love felt safe and sacred for those forty-eight hours.

Following a Sacred Path

Sometimes your honeymoon offers a richer adventure in the spiritual dimension than you might have planned on or foreseen. When Phila and Erick announced their engagement and Phila's father, a Catholic, learned that Erick was Quaker, divorced, eleven years older than Phila, and had a daughter, he disapproved. At first Phila was devastated. But as time moved along and she became closer to Erick's family, she realized that she was following the "Golden Thread," as Robert Johnson calls an unexpected opening or magical intervention that leads you in a new direction — even when it stems from something "negative." Phila told us:

As a result of my father's disapproving withdrawal, I became more aware of and drawn to Erick's Quaker history. We chose, for emotional and financial reasons, to spend our honeymoon touring his family's point of origin in the United States: nearby Chester County, Pennsylvania, where the first Hoopes family had settled after emigrating with William Penn.

We started at the three-hundred-year-old family homestead, which is now a B and B, and then spent a night or two at all the other family historic sites in the area. A clairvoyant friend said that he saw our ancestors' spirits with us at our wedding. And we certainly felt them with us as we visited their territory throughout the honeymoon.

Sensing the ancestors, especially at Brooznoll (the family's first home), really anchored in Erick and me the sense that "Yes, this was meant to be."

Once-in-a-Lifetime Trips

Cynthia's honeymoon "was very romantic, a once-in-a-lifetime thrill. We traveled to Hawaii, Tahiti, New Zealand, Australia, and Fiji for six weeks on a hundred dollars. I was working for the airlines as a travel specialist, which meant the entire airfare was free and the hotel rooms were complimentary. It was truly a fairy-tale adventure."

Her husband, Brian, said, "We flew to the island of Mooréa, where we were given a thatched hut on the whitest sand with the aqua-blue ocean steps from the door. We went scuba diving, canoeing, hiking, and swimming, and it was the most romantic place ever. We both felt so blessed that we could experience this magical beauty together."

Cynthia added, "Each destination was a joy. Even when we locked ourselves out of our rental car, we laughed. Attitude is everything!"

Brian explained, "At the time, I didn't realize what a gift it was to have six weeks of travel for almost no money. I had just graduated from dental school and was twenty-five thousand dollars in debt and anxious to get to work. Cynthia kept saying, 'We'll never have this opportunity again; we need to appreciate every moment.' She was right. In twenty-nine years of marriage, the longest vacation we've managed since is two weeks away from home. As I look back, I wish I had listened to her and continued traveling for another month."

Cynthia had one more thing to say. "We know now that once a person starts a career, family, owns a home, etc., responsibilities mount and the chance to just pick up and wander the world diminishes. If we could give one word of advice to newlyweds, it would be to take as much time as possible to discover the marvels around you while you can."

Testing Your Love

Nothing is supposed to spoil your honeymoon fun. You expect to be in perfect harmony. Yet the oddest things happen to test your love, sometimes by "accident," and sometimes just because.

Patrick and Gayle went to a private island in the Caribbean. The first day was a wonder of snorkeling, lying on the beach, and making love. The second day, Patrick had to get a prescription for the pain of his second-degree sunburn, and he could barely move for the next two days. "I was furious," Gayle confided. "How could Patrick be so stupid and not use my sunblock? How could he spoil our honeymoon?"

"But," Patrick said, "when I reluctantly talked with her about how ashamed and embarrassed I felt, and how afraid I was that she might leave me for being such a fool, she was wonderful."

"I realized that he was being very intimate in telling me that. In fact, never before then had I seen him be so vulnerable. I got sort of choked up and told him how much closer I felt."

"Who knew that a dumb sunburn could be so romantic?" Patrick laughed. Not only didn't it spoil their time away, but they came home with a richer commitment to their relationship. Gayle had new respect for Patrick's tenderness, and Patrick had new respect for Gayle's compassion — as well as her capacity to entertain herself while he was incapacitated.

On the second day of our honeymoon in Paris, Judith's left ankle developed a peculiar sensitivity to her well-worn Reeboks. (The left side of the body is generally understood to represent the feminine, receptive part of our nature.) What had been a perfectly comfortable shoe became persistently abrasive. In short, it hurt. As we walked around, she complained about the weird pain and the raw feeling under her sock. So, from a street vendor, I bought her another pair of socks. The double layer helped a bit.

But the next day, as we went in and out of beautiful cathedrals and strolled down tree-lined boulevards, Judith still complained about her ankle, so much so that she began to feel guilty that she was spoiling my fun.

In a little bistro, over a lunch of escargots, Judith made a frantic announcement. "I'm going to go home. You stay here. I don't want to wreck this trip for you, and this stuff with my ankle is driving me crazy. Just take me to the airport and..."

"That's crazy," I blurted. "Absolutely not. We're going to get Band-Aids and tape, and you're going to be fine. You're not leaving." We went down the block to the pharmacy, and I bought all manner of tape and stretch bandages. I sat her down on an outdoor stairway, took off her shoe, taped her ankle, and put back her double set of socks. Even though the irritation didn't entirely leave until we were back in the States, we walked around the city and had a wonderful time.

It's true that Judith got a little nutty. But like many people, she grew up feeling that her needs were annoying to her parents. She didn't believe that she could be taken care of. In retrospect, it was no surprise that the ankle problem, which had never occurred before and hasn't occurred since, was her way of expressing her inability to fully trust the joy and beauty she was experiencing. Unconsciously, Judith, needed to test herself, me, and the happiness she felt, and the pain in her ankle represented her resistance to our honeyed-moon.

I'm glad to say that I passed the test with flying bandages. And Judith gained a new depth of faith in the love she had finally found.

Making the Most of Your Moods

Paige and JC had planned to go to the Seychelles Islands, off the coast of Africa, for their honeymoon. But, as Paige told us:

9/11 happened and we changed our minds. Traveling that far from the United States just didn't feel right. So we decided on Las Alamandas, in Mexico, and it was the best thing we could have done! We had a week to ourselves on a beautiful beach, and it was only two and a half hours' flying time from Colorado. We laughed at how crazy we had been to plan a trip halfway around the world right after our wedding. A honeymoon was not the time for us to explore a foreign country. We were exhausted and spent the first three days in bed or playing cards in our room.

Despite the advertising that suggests you'll feel only free and joyous, we were both terribly sad that the wedding weekend was over. It really felt like a loss. We had put an entire year into planning, and it was hard to accept that it had come and gone, never to be repeated.

The sadness hit me first when we were in the airport picking out magazines for the flight to Mexico. I realized that I would never have a reason to buy another bridal magazine. I'd consumed dozens of them. I had loved them and looked forward to getting them. But there in the airport I knew that part of my life was over.

JC and I overcame our sadness on the honeymoon by replaying with each other all our memories from the wedding. We asked each other: "What was your favorite part? What was your least favorite part? When were you happiest? When were you most tired? What would you do differently?" And on and on. We spent the entire week rehashing the wedding, which allowed us to relive all of the special moments and learn a thing or two about each other's memories and experiences. Like I said before, we still find rehashing the wedding a complete joy and look forward to our chicken potpie dates so that we have an excuse to talk about it!

The Wedding Memories Game

Inspired by Paige and JC, you might want to take the following list with you on your honeymoon and play the wedding memories game, too. Ask each other the following questions and any others that come to mind. Remember, you will have had different experiences and different perceptions of the same events, so there's no reason to disagree. Use this time to learn more about each other and to rejoice in the magic of your memories!

❖ *What was your favorite part of the wedding?*

❖ *What was your least favorite part?*

❖ *What was the most romantic moment?*

❖ *When were you most moved or choked up?*

❖ *When were you happiest?*

❖ *When were you most tired?*

❖ *Which were the most touching congratulations you received?*

❖ *Who surprised you with unexpected support and happiness for us?*

❖ *Who was most fun at the reception?*

❖ *Which toast did you like best?*

❖ *What would you do differently?*

❖ *Which moment would you most like to live over again?*

Your Emotional Adventure

For most couples, honeymoons can be emotional roller coasters. Romance, sex, exhaustion, and even anxiety about your new status as newlyweds fight for your attention. Just when you feel amorous, your new wife is caught up feeling guilty about this or that moment that didn't go well at the reception. Right about the time you're leaving for a wonderfully elegant dinner, your husband is overcome with raging turista. You discover, despite how well you thought you knew each other, that he feels compelled to call in to work each day or that she wants to make friends with another couple in your hotel when you want her all to yourself. Yet, despite the fact that such issues are common, they are not at all part of the lure and lore of the honeymoon.

But as long as you keep your focus on the well-being of your relationship, you'll have an emotionally intimate time no matter what happens. When you understand how the events of your special day might impact you, you'll anticipate that your honeymoon could include intimate sharing about your darker feelings, your letdown, or your fears about being together in an ordinary, postgala, day-to-day life. Of course, there'll also be wonderful fun and fascinating discoveries, but this time of decompression sets the stage — emotionally and spiritually — for how you'll jointly handle all the ups and downs of the many years to come. And the tenderness of this revealing time — from the "dark side of the moon" — will be the true blessing as you begin your marriage!

Our Wish for You

Your marriage, a sacred home for your hearts to share,
is yours to design and evolve. It is not ever settled, not ever to be
taken for granted, but explored as you would explore outer space.
Only now it is inner space that you have entered, given
yourselves to, and committed to for a lifetime.

Our wish for you — each of you — is that you will willingly go
where love leads you. Of course, you will face challenging times,
both from within your relationship as well as coming from
the outside world. But when you surrender to the spiritual and
emotional growth that love has in store for you, you can be
grateful, fully available to all that the two of you will share.

Hold each other's hearts with tender care and stay open to all that
is being born between you. Ride the passions of your souls, and
awaken in your marriage bed filled with wonder that you
have found each other, that you have made your way together,
and that you are now, in fact, truly home.

Index

About the Authors

*H*usband-and-wife psychology team Judith Sherven, PhD, and James Sniechowski, PhD, are among the country's most respected and pioneering authorities on turning the challenges of intimate relationship into successful marriage and life-long romance.

They are the bestselling authors of *Be Loved for Who You Really Are* (St. Martin's Press, 2003), *The New Intimacy* (Health Communications, 1997), and *Opening to Love 365 Days a Year* (Health Communications, 2000). They are dynamic speakers who provide workshops, teleseminars, keynote addresses, and corporate trainings.

As guest experts, they have appeared on more than nine hundred television and talk-radio shows, including *Oprah, The O'Reilly Factor, The View, 48 Hours, Canada AM, MSNBC,* and *CNN.* They have been interviewed for and published by hundreds of newspapers and magazines, including the *Los Angeles*

Times, USA Today, the Chicago Tribune, O, Family Circle, Redbook, Cosmopolitan, Glamour, Playboy, Woman's Day, and *Parents Magazine,* and they are columnists for *Today's Black Woman.*

They were both involved in the film industry earlier in their lives, Judith as an actress, Jim as an actor, director, and teacher. They have worked nationally and internationally for the last seventeen years as relationship trainers and motivational speakers and they know what men and women need in order to create satisfaction and success in their marriages.

They both love to travel, dance, and hike around the country hills where they live. They can often be found at local antique auctions or searching for choice bargains at yard sales. For Judith and Jim, life is an adventure filled with mysteries and discoveries, and they each say that the best discovery was meeting each other in 1987 — on a blind date.

They love joyous, meaningful weddings and thoroughly enjoyed creating their own in 1988. More than their extensive professional backgrounds, Judith and Jim bring profound personal experience and knowledge to their work. They have been married for seventeen years. It's Judith's first and Jim's third marriage, so they bring hope for almost everyone!

Connect with Judith & Jim

Visit Judith and Jim's websites, www.themagicofdifferences .com and www.smartcoupleswedding.com, where you can subscribe to any of their free e-zines:

Smart Dating
Smart Wedding Couples
Letting Love Lead
Your Optimal Workplace

On their websites you can also learn about their various workshops, teleseminars, and many other services for singles and couples as well as for businesses, associations, nonprofits, and educational organizations.

If you want to contact Judith and Jim to book them for a media event or a talk or workshop in your area or to discuss other possibilities, email them at judithandjim@judithandjim.com.